D1736186

Sermons That Work V:

Distinctive Dimensions
in Anglican Preaching

edited by

Roger Alling
and
David J. Schlafer

Forward Movement Publications
Cincinnati, Ohio

Contents

Sacraments and Sacred Metaphors

A Social Center for Spiritual Discernment

The Winners of the Fifth Annual Competition

The Rev. J. Donald Waring of St. Thomas' Church, Terrace Park, Ohio

The Rev. Richard I.H. Belser of St. Michael's Church, Charleston, South Carolina

The Rev. Andrew C. Hamersley of St. Andrew's Church, Albany, New York

The Rev. Edward Garrigan of Saint Paul's Church, Doylestown, Pennsylvania

The Rev. Karen Siegfriedt of Saint Luke's Church, Los Gatos, California

The Rev. Glenn E. Busch of Saint Mary's Church, High Point, North Carolina

The Rev. Bruce Shortell of The Cathedral of Saint Philip, Atlanta, Georgia

The Rev. Robert Hirschfeld of Saint Mark's Episcopal Chapel, Storrs, Connecticut

The Rev. James G. Bradley of Saint John's Church, Waterbury, Connecticut

The Rev. Jennifer Phillips of Trinity Parish, Saint Louis, Missouri

Foreword

Controversy rages in the Episcopal Church at the national, diocesan, and parish levels. Let us hope that the end result is renewed spirit, vigor, and understanding, but regardless, one thing is clear. The views of many Episcopalians will not be considered because they are not participating in the debates. These are the church's alumni, that vast throng that find the church of so little relevance that they have abandoned it except possibly for Christmas, Easter, baptisms, weddings, and funerals.

Many aspects of the church can be relevant to people's lives—fellowship, music, youth programs, and certainly good preaching. Many alumni would re-enroll if the gospel were consistently preached in lively and meaningful ways. The mission of the Episcopal Evangelism Foundation is to promote and encourage just such excellent preaching.

Each year all parishes in the church are invited to submit sermons preached recently by their clergy. The entries are judged by the Foundation's Board of Directors, and the top five winners, as well as their parishes, are awarded cash prizes, generously donated by Mr. John C. Whitehead, former Deputy Secretary of State and an active Episcopalian. This year's winning sermons, as well as the five runners-up, are printed here.

Also included are sermons and addresses delivered by the faculty at our eighth annual Preaching Excellence Conference, held in June, 1995, in Washington,

D.C. Each year nearly 50 seminarians who show out-standing promise in preaching are selected by the deans and homiletics professors of all eleven Episcopal seminaries. They spend an intensive week on the art and practice of preaching, led by five homiletics profes-sors and five skilled parish preachers in addition to well known guest lecturers including, this year, Associate Supreme Court Justice Sandra Day O'Connor.

As you read these sermons, and especially if you compare them with those similarly published in the four preceding years, we hope you will agree that preaching in the Episcopal Church is improving. Fur-thermore, it gets more and more difficult each year to select the winners from among many fine submissions. Maybe our Best Sermon Competition is growing in reputation and attracting better entries, but I also believe that the general quality of sermons is rising.

Nevertheless, there is still plenty of room for im-provement. Please help us encourage excellent Episco-pal preaching with your comments and with your tax deductible dollars. Most of all, we hope this book helps you in a concrete way in your own spiritual journey.

A. Gary Shilling
Chairman,
The Episcopal Evangelism Foundation
500 Morris Avenue
Springfield, NJ 07081

Is There Anything Distinctive About *Anglican* Preaching?

"Not particularly," some would say—"nor should there be."

Those who make this claim can set forth a clear case. "Preaching is simply *preaching,*" they assert, "because the gospel is the gospel." They can cite no less an authority than the Apostle Paul. "In Christ there is no longer Jew or Greek, slave or free, male or female," Paul tells the Galatians, "for all of you are one in Christ Jesus."

If that is so, the argument runs, then in Christ there is no longer Presbyterian, Roman Catholic, Baptist, or Episcopalian either. Denominations are an embarrassing witness to the scandal of our "sad divisions" as Christians. To define the preaching of one faith tradition in distinction from others only exacerbates the wounds of a Body that needs to spend its energy working toward healing and, as much as possible, manifesting the ideal of its God-given wholeness.

"Is there anything distinctive about *Anglican* preaching?"

"Not particularly"—a disconcertingly corroborating claim is sometimes posed from a different quarter. "Anglicans don't have anything of substance to contribute to the preaching enterprise."

Whatever its merits, the perception is pronounced.

"What would an *Anglican* teacher of preaching have to offer our students?" That was a question recently asked over and over of an Episcopal homiletics professor during interviews for a faculty vacancy at a large protestant seminary. The operating assumption in the question seemed to be that a characteristic Anglican concern with liturgy and the Eucharist would seriously distract—in fact, if not in intent—from serious attention (and distinctive contribution) to "the ministry of the word."

During the late sixties and early seventies there was, in fact, a significant upsurge of commitment to preaching in the Episcopal seminaries. That brief period, however, has been followed by severe retrenchment (as Roger Alling notes in his contribution to this volume). If proportion is any indication of priority as far as professional theological resources are concerned, then perhaps it is not unfair to say that Episcopalians are losing their sense of heritage and identity in respect to preaching.

Yet it would be misleading to conclude that Episcopalians are not concerned about preaching—preaching of a distinctive kind. "Effective preacher" consistently ranks first, or very near the top in the stated priorities of parishes seeking new clergy. Pressed further, individuals will speak of how they were attracted to the Episcopal Church, not only because of the liturgical emphasis, but also because the preaching was "different."

Members of Episcopal congregations may not always be able to articulate succinctly what they want (or what they need) in a preacher—but they know very clearly, and say rather loudly that they want "good preaching"—and not just preaching per se, but preaching that is deeply rooted in a distinctive and vital heritage.

What, if anything, about an *Anglican* sermon distinguishes and commends it? The question could be posed in a spirit of competition with other religious denominations; but it does not have to be. It can rather be posed in a spirit of collegiality: What special gifts has this tradition received? How do they distinctively stimulate and support the broader preaching conversations of the larger church? How does Episcopal preaching contribute to the upbuilding of the Body of Christ?

This small volume, the fifth in an annual series, responds to these constructive questions with seventeen sermons that "show and tell" the riches of Anglican preaching, conveying something of its variety and its energy. These are not essays *about* preaching; they are "sermons that work"—preaching that came to life initially in particular congregational settings, but that still resounds in this secondary, more reflective printed format.

What you will see and hear as you read and listen is, of course, fundamentally and finally an act of privileged communication among you, the sermon's author, and God's Spirit. It may be helpful, however, with the question of "Anglican distinctives" in mind, to pause briefly before plunging into the preaching conversation that these sermons convene. What, particularly, do we want to be attentive to in the listening process? What sorts of things are we listening for? What explicitly does preaching in the Episcopal tradition *sound* like?

In these sermons you will hear a great deal of scripture—not proof texts bumper-stickered at strategic intervals, and not verse-by-verse exposition, commentary, and application. You will, however, in practically every sermon, hear scripture seriously engaged as a significant partner in the unfolding process of sermon dialogue. Yet this in itself is not distinctively

Anglican. (Indeed, it should not be—it is, rather, distinctively *Christian.*) You will hear much of a reforming, regenerating, recreative relationship with God through faith in Jesus Christ. But this too, obviously, has been the common thrust of gospel preaching since Peter's first sermon at Pentecost.

What you will hear that is distinctive, we think (and if you have spent length of days in an Episcopal church, this may be so familiar that you will need to "taste it again for the first time") is preaching that is not only grounded in scripture, and focused on the saving activity of Jesus Christ, but also shaped by an interplay of three additional dimensions:

1) Seasons and special days
2) Sacraments and sacred metaphors
3) A social center for spiritual discernment.

Effective Anglican preaching does not talk *about* seasons, sacraments, or social issues as such. Rather, it uses these as lenses through which to look at experiences of God's saving grace as recorded in scripture, and encountered in relationship with Christ—lenses, or lights that play upon the many layered mystery of God's love. We will have more to say about each of these dimensions as they are unfolded in the following pages.

The categories we have chosen as an organizational framework are not sharp-edged. (We use the words "dimension" and "interplay" in the paragraph before last advisedly.) Two of the sermons we have included here were preached on Ember Days. One we have subsumed under the "Seasons and Special Days" heading, the other under "Sacraments and Sacred Metaphors." Each might, with justification, be incorporated under the other heading—or, for that matter, under the "Social Center for Spiritual Discernment" section. The choice represents only the hermeneutical "judgment call" of the two editors in this particular context.

It will be quickly evident that the sermon styles, theological perspectives, and particular uses of scripture, reason, and experience employed by these preachers differ widely. We suspect, however, that the careful listener to all of these sermons will discern underneath these widely varied celebrations of preaching ministry a family resemblance, and a common resonance that is both clear and distinctive. While abstract homiletical generalizations are often not worth the trouble it takes for the reader to plow through (or for the author/editor to construct!), actual sermon instances, gently shaped in their presentation, may rather palpably convey a clear impression: "Yes, *this* is the flavor of preaching in the Anglican tradition. It is distinctive and savory. The nourishment as well as the flavor is significant." We hope that you find this to be the case as you taste the riches of God's grace through these sermons in the Anglican tradition.

The sermons we have included come from two different sources. Ten were first preached in parishes, and were selected by the Episcopal Evangelism Foundation from many entries submitted from across the country as sermons particularly representative of excellent preaching in the Episcopal tradition. The other seven sermons were preached by professional staff leaders at the annual Excellence in Preaching Conference, where selected Episcopal seminary students are given an intensive week of support, prior to ordination, for their developing preaching vocation.

Seasons and Special Days

The first-timer to an Episcopal worship service almost-inevitably stumbles (and is sometimes overwhelmed by) a formidable array of apparent ecclesiastical intricacy.

It is not just that the order of worship itself seems complicated. In addition to negotiating that complexity, the worshiper is also sent scurrying off to various corners of the prayer book and service leaflets in search of prayers, scripture passages, and worship patterns that "are appointed" for this day, and for no other.

The assault on the consciousness of the uninitiated is in some ways worse than having to contend with an inscrutable set of directions from the IRS. Faced with numerous books and bulletins, and with constantly changing directions for standing, sitting, and kneeling, the Episcopal worshiper must also be adept at hand-body-brain-eye-coordination—and all this in the presence of God and an assembled company of other people who give the impression that *they* know what they are doing!

"How essential is all of this to the worship of God?" the fumbling worshiper wonders. Explanation is needed as well as direction. But if the needed directions *do* come, either in cues and asides throughout the service, or in extended discussions during the sermon, the effect can be as distracting from worship as getting no direction at all. In a word, constant talk *in* the service about what we are *doing* in the service is not unlike what would happen in the theater if the actors recited the stage directions written in their scripts along with their lines of dramatic dialogue.

At its worst, then, a worship focus directed *to* seasons and special days will more than likely prevent the congregation from worshiping *through* these special observances, and the particular liturgical patterns laid out for these occasions.

Effectively undertaken by a skilled and sensitive worship leader, however, specially designated prayers, readings, and worship patterns can help those who gather for praise and petition to *experience* the fact (not just *reflect on* the fact) that, while God's presence is a gracious, unremitting Given, the *manifestation* of this presence is always fresh and specific to the hour.

Just as we always want to be remembered on our birthdays, but sort of want to be surprised as well, so, in worship, we want to encounter a *dependable* "God of surprises." Providing, in liturgy and preaching, for liturgical seasons and special days is one way Episcopalians make advance preparation for God's trustworthy but unpredictable coming to us in ways that are distinctively relevant to our experiences here and now.

The sermons in this section are an unsystematic sampling of how God's special grace can be celebrated on particular occasions. The season or special day, in each case, shapes the preaching event. This shaping is clear but subtle—somewhat more explicit in some of the sermons than in others.

Donald Waring presents the Advent call for active anticipation of Divine presence, which God's prophets have sounded throughout salvation history, as an urgent invitation to "get in character." What does "preparing the way of the Lord" have to do with the intensive, selfless character study a good actor undertakes before performing a role in a play? An unfolding of that intriguing notion is the journey of this Advent sermon.

How does one undertake the state of "suspended animation" that waiting for God almost always entails? **Neil Alexander** explores the feel of that in his sermon for the Eve of Pentecost, in which he captures the tension that disciples in every age undergo as they await an outpouring of God's Spirit that is *promised*, but *not yet*.

What do the embarrassments and infirmities of portly old age have to do with spiritual health and healing? The Feast of the Transfiguration provides **Edward Carrigan** with an ideal opportunity for a theologically seasoned offering of pastoral care.

How can a celebration of Anglican heritage, such as is provided for in the Lesser Feast designated as "The First Book of Common Prayer"—"appropriately observed on a weekday following the Day of Pentecost"— be an occasion of humility, gratitude, and challenge rather than an occasion for getting denominationally ostentatious? **David Schlafer** undertakes that assignment, along with offering a new reading of the Fourth Gospel's familiar story of Jesus' encounter with the woman at the well.

Ember Day, a celebration of ministry in the church, gives **Judith McDaniel**, in "What You See Is What You Get," an opportunity to look at ministry in categories that are spiritually more meaningful because they are sociologically and psychologically mundane, rather than abstractly theological "church talk."

In all of these sermons, you will see that the season or the occasion serves as a window on the Gospel; but also that the creative vision of the preacher has been brought to bear as well, both on the occasion and on the scriptures which are designated for the occasion.

What makes for a lively experience of grace, in other words, requires a particular occasion, but it also requires more than a published liturgical calendar and a set of rubrics. It requires the imagination of a preacher that is sensitive to seasons of grace.

Getting in Character

*As it is written in the book of the words of
Isaiah the prophet, "The voice of one crying in
the wilderness: Prepare ye the way of the
Lord, make his paths straight."*   —Luke 3:4

My one and only flirtation with the stage occurred when I was in the third grade, and played the role of a decayed tooth during dental hygiene week. Not so with my younger brother, however. Throughout high school and college, he tried out for and won a number of significant roles in the theater. His first character portrayal was that of the doctor in "Whose Life is it Anyway?" He brought to the role a stern, strident, unyielding presence. And although my credibility as a theater critic is not high, I was quite impressed. His next role was Captain Brackett in the musical "South Pacific." He brought to the role a stern, strident, unyielding presence. I thought to myself, "Hmm, this looks familiar." Then came his portrayals of John Proctor in "The Crucible," and Dwight Babcock in "Mame." To these roles he brought a stern, strident, unyielding presence. Perhaps the problem was my own perception. Perhaps it was because I knew my brother too well, but it seemed to me that he was playing the same character no matter what costume he wore, no matter what lines he spoke.

One day in the spirit of helpfulness I broached the subject of his need to take more of the character into himself; let the character shape you as much as you shape the character. Get yourself more out of the way. To these brotherly criticisms he responded by saying that since it wasn't dental hygiene week I ought to consider shutting my mouth. A rather stern, strident, and unyielding answer, don't you think?

> *Prepare ye the way of the Lord, make his paths straight.*

What do these familiar words mean? We hear them often during the season of Advent. Three-hundred years ago George Frederic Handel set them to music, as countless others have done since. Two thousand years ago John the Baptist spoke them in the wilderness of Judea, and on the banks of the Jordan River. But even then the words were not new; the people to whom John spoke had heard them before many times. The words were a familiar portion of the Hebrew Scriptures. They were read in the synagogue. But what did they mean?

Some five hundred years before John, Isaiah the prophet first spoke these words. Isaiah preached good news to the people in exile. The Jews were captives in Babylon; the Babylonians had conquered them and carried them away from Jerusalem. For decades now they had languished in Babylonian internment camps, all the while mourning their separation from Jerusalem. How could they play the role of God's people if they didn't live in God's city? *How shall we sing the Lord's song in a strange land?* (Psalm 137). By the waters of Babylon they sat down and wept: their costumes didn't fit; the props were all wrong; the scenery wasn't right. Then came Isaiah speaking words of comfort:

> *Comfort ye, comfort ye my people, saith your God. Speak ye comfortably to Jerusalem, and*

*cry unto her, that her warfare is accomplished,
that her iniquity is pardoned: for she hath
received of the Lord's hand double for all
her sins. The voice of him that crieth in the
wilderness, Prepare ye the way of the Lord,
make straight in the desert a highway for
our God.* —Isaiah 40

For the Jews this meant that they would be going
home. The way they would have to travel from Babylon
to Jerusalem was long and treacherous. The most
direct route was across 600 miles of desert. The more
hospitable route was close to 900 miles. Mountains,
valleys, rough places and rough people would block
their way. But God himself was going to prepare the
way.

Two thousand, five hundred years ago, that was the
meaning of these words. God brought the Jews home
again to Jerusalem. The city was in ruins; the Temple
was destroyed. But they were home. The trouble was,
though, Jerusalem turned out to be not at all the
heaven on earth they remembered. They were in the
right place, they wore the right costumes, they spoke
the right lines, but those who felt distant from God in
Babylon still felt distant from God in Jerusalem. "Hmm,"
they must have thought, "this feels familiar." A change
of scenery wasn't the answer.

*Prepare ye the way of the Lord, make his
paths straight. Every valley shall be filled, and
every mountain and hill shall be brought low;
and the crooked shall be made straight, and
the rough ways shall be made smooth.*

What do these words mean? When John the Baptist
spoke them again five hundred years after Isaiah, he

7

brought a stern, strident, unyielding presence to the role of a prophet. His were not words of comfort. The great distance he spoke of was not that between Babylon and Jerusalem; it was the distance between our thoughts and God's thoughts, between our ways and God's ways. The mountains, valleys, and rough places he referred to were not that of any outward landscape, but rather the untamed geography of the inner life. John preached a baptism of repentance for the forgiveness of sins. That's a fancy way of talking about a change of character, not a change of scenery. We will sing a hymn today which says it well:

> Then cleansed be every breast from sin;
> make straight the way for God within. And let
> each heart prepare a home where such a
> mighty guest may come.   —Hymn 76

Make straight the way for God within. I heard a phrase this week which I think is a good one, and which fits here. It goes like this: "The Christian journey is not so much a matter of getting people into heaven later on, as it is getting heaven into people now." Did you catch that: not people into heaven, but heaven into people. How in the world does this happen? Well, this is a journey that God makes. Now to say that God makes the journey goes against the fashion of the day, which urges me to concentrate on my spiritual journey, and you on yours. "We are all on a spiritual journey," is what you hear over and over again. We are all busy wanting out of Babylon and longing for Jerusalem.

To be sure, we do some spiritual wandering here and there. But the one on the spiritual journey is God. His destination is your inner depths, and mine—your heart and mine. Let every heart prepare a home where such a mighty guest may come. Prepare ye the way of the Lord!

These ancient, familiar words present a challenge to me which I think is not unlike the challenge before an actor or actress portraying a character. To prepare the way of the Lord is to learn a character—the character of Christ. If you have ever been in a play, you know that to some extent you have to get yourself out of the way; not every mountain and valley and rough place of your personality is fit for the stage; it is a matter of letting the character shape you as much as you shaping the character. It is an integration of persons in which neither is lost totally in the other. This is what St. Paul meant when he talked about "putting on Christ" (Romans 13:14), and "having the mind of Christ" (1 Corinthians 2:16), and Christ "being formed in us" (Galatians 4:19). We heard this in the Collect of the Day last week, when we prayed that God would "give us grace that we may cast away the works of darkness, and put upon us the armor or light, now in the time of this mortal life . . . " We hear this each week in the Eucharistic Prayer, when we pray to God that we may "be filled with thy grace and heavenly benediction, and made one body with him, that he may dwell in us, and we in him."

Prepare ye the way of the Lord! Put on Christ. Get into character. Remember that we are each playing the role of Christ in the drama of our lives: we are his ambassadors, we are representing him to the world. Stage directors will tell their performers to stay in character no matter what happens, no matter what props fall over, or what lines are flubbed. The question is, will we stay in character? When the pressures of life mount and your temper wears thin, will you stay in the character of Christ? When you face major decisions about money and morals, will you stay in the character of Christ? When you've heard an irresistible piece of gossip at a Christmas party, and now have the chance to repeat it, will you break character with Christ, or will you consider shutting your mouth? When someone cuts you off on the highway, and then perhaps flips you off, will you stay in the character of Christ, or will your old self win out?

It sounds like an impossible role to play, a task even more difficult than traveling from Babylon to Jerusalem. But remember, God is the one on the move toward us. God is the one who first gives himself to us. God in Christ has acted to take our nature upon himself—to play our role, to stand in our place. And here I can only say what I have found to be true: that the more I am willing to let the character of Christ shape me, rather than vice versa, the more I know the Spirit of God alive in me. The more I take on the role of Christ, the more that role becomes part of my nature. And the more that role becomes part of my nature, the more I realize that God is working infinitely harder than I ever could in the transformation of my character. He has begun a good work within each of us, and he will perform it until the day of Jesus Christ. He is planning to give us his resurrected life, so that we might say, "It is no longer I who live, but Christ who lives in me" (Galatians 2:20).

Once again, let me say that my credibility as a theater critic is not all that high. It is not even dental hygiene week. But it is Advent. So I tell you: Take the character of Christ into yourself. Receive his body and blood. Receive his forgiveness, and healing, and call to ministry. Let him shape you.

Prepare ye the way of the Lord, make his paths straight. Every valley shall be filled, and

every mountain and hill shall be brought low,
and the crooked shall be made straight, and
the rough ways shall be made smooth; and all
flesh shall see the salvation of God.

Let them see it in you, and let them see it in me.
Amen.

The Rev. J. Donald Waring

Living in the Middle of the Story

Be still. Listen. Don't be too anxious. Wait. Things take time. Don't be in such a hurry. If you're not careful you may miss it. Ssh. Be still. Listen. Wait.

The vigil readings for the Eve of Pentecost, for the first Eucharist of Easter's jubilee, are readings that call us to draw in closer, readings that raise our expectations, that tighten and pull at us like the calm before the storm. It is the deep breath before the final shout of unbridled rejoicing.

It wasn't really that long ago: we followed a pillar of cloud by day and a pillar of fire by night; we sang Exultet; we heard redemption's story; we heard the roaring hooves and felt the mighty splash of the horse and its rider; we made new friends in a candlelit bath and lavished their bodies with salvation's salve, and our cup ran over with love. Alleluia!

Life was full because the grave was empty. It was a long night of waiting, longing, hoping, expecting, wanting more than anything else to get on with it. Yet knowing deep within that joy comes in the morning, that the moment is not yet, and that the best is here and still to come.

Horton Foote, the great American playwright, said, "I existed before I was born because of the stories I was told." And in another place, he wrote, "I was born into the middle of the story." The Eve of Pentecost is a good time to celebrate the grace of being born into the middle of the story. Because of the stories we have been told we have seen the future, we have tasted the promise, the

Spirit of God is upon us we are chosen and we are changed!

But we are also tired. Travel weary. Seminary weary. Spiritually weary. I would love to believe that my weariness is the direct result of being tuckered out from fifty days of a non-stop, on-my-feet, unrestrained resurrection jamboree.

But what I also know is that I have not forgotten some other things. I have not forgotten Oklahoma City. Nor Sarajevo. Nor Belfast. I have not forgotten Nicole and Ron. Nor O.J. I have not forgotten Bishop Johnson. Nor Bishop Browning. I have not forgotten two of my students and friends who were faithful priests of this church and both of whom were taken from us recently by AIDS.

I could go on and on. You could add your pain to my list and we could talk and sip until dawn and blather about how bad things are and how much worse they are going to get.

OR, we can wallow in the promising grace of being born into the middle of the story.

Remember that valley of dry, parched bones? Remember the tired and weary people of God? Remember their longing? Remember how much hope they wanted to have but simply couldn't will it on their own?

Remember the promise? The bones will rattle with life; the bones will jump for joy; the Spirit of God will blow over those bones and they will come together full of energy, covered in flesh, brimming with new life?

Yours, ours, is the grace of living in the middle of the story. "The sufferings of this present time are not worth comparing with the glory about to be revealed to us." (Romans 8:18)

Come, Holy Spirit, come.

The Rev. J. Neil Alexander, Th.D.

Changed into His Likeness

Lesson: 1 Kings 19:9-18   Gospel: Mark 9:2-9

From today's Collect:

> *Grant that we, beholding by faith the light of his countenance . . . may be changed into his likeness from glory to glory . . .*

"Changed into his likeness . . . " I want to tell you about an old friend of mine, now long dead. Her name was Nell Frommelt. She and her husband, Andrew, had been founding members—the most prominent of the founding members—of the congregation fifty years earlier.

Now nearly ninety, they lived two doors away from the rectory in the house in which they had lived their almost seventy years of marriage and in which their three children—they, now, in their sixties—had been born.

More than parishioners, Nell and Andrew were neighbors, friends, and—maybe most importantly—staunch supporters of the young, green rector in his first parish.

I saw them often. And one day Nell suddenly asked me, "Rector"—that's what she always called me—"Rector, when people get to heaven, do they recognize one another?"

My first thought: "How should I know?" I kept that one to myself! My second thought: that usual response about being so caught up in the glory of seeing Jesus that we won't care about recognizing one another. I kept that to myself as well. I knew it wouldn't fly. Nell wanted an answer. If not an answer from the Bible, then at least the rector's considered opinion—on a subject the rector hadn't considered.

Now you would assume, I suppose, that a ninety-year-old woman, in somewhat failing health, with a husband she clearly loved even more that day than the day they were married, and three children of whom she was, quite rightly, proud, was looking for the assurance that yes, indeed, in heaven she and Andrew and their children would all recognize one another.

That's what I assumed. I was dead wrong.

I found out that day something I hadn't known before. Upstairs in the big front bedroom, Nell had given birth to five children, not three. Twin girls, born prematurely, had lived only a few days.

Now you need to know that, in appearance, Nell was a cross between an elephant—that being roughly the texture of her skin—and a battleship on maneuvers—that being her heft and carriage. She resembled a cartoonist's grande dame.

Nell's greatest fear—she had no fear at all of dying—her greatest fear—and she was in absolute earnest about this—was that she would go to heaven and those two precious babies would see what a wrinkled old warrior their young mother had become!

The answer she was looking for was not "yes," but "no," in heaven people do not recognize one another.

I didn't know whether to laugh or cry. But if I'd been quicker on my feet, I hope that by way of a reply I would have pointed Nell to today's Gospel and its vision of Jesus transfigured. I say that because it has finally dawned on me that in this transfiguration Gospel I've all along been missing the most obvious thing of all.

We talk about this vision of Jesus transfigured as God's merciful and gracious gift to the disciples: *arming them* against despair in the coming terrors of Jerusalem and dereliction of Calvary. Arming them with a foretaste—actually, a foresight—of the triumphant, risen Jesus they shall meet after Easter on the road to Emmaus, or in the upper room, or on the beach at dawn.

And as Episcopalians—for whom liturgy is next to godliness—we talk about how the arrangers of the lectionary give *us* this vision of Jesus transfigured in glory every year on this last Sunday before Ash Wednesday, *arming us* with the foresight of the Easter Jesus before we, with ashes and fasting, begin to walk towards Jerusalem with him.

And we talk about the vision of Jesus transfigured as a portrait of Jesus as we shall see him on the other side of our own deaths, when, as the Advent hymn puts it:

> *Those dear tokens of his passion*
> *still his dazzling body bears,*
> *cause of endless exultation*
> *to his ransomed worshipers.*
>
> —Hymn 57

But what I have failed to notice, until this year, is that the transfigured Jesus is not only a portrait of him when we shall see him, *it is also a portrait of us* when, as the Collect says, we shall "be changed into his likeness from glory to glory;" when, as Paul tells the Corinthians, "this corruptible shall have put on incorruption, and this mortal shall have put on immortality, and death is swallowed up in victory"; when, as Paul tells the Colossians, "we shall appear with him in glory."

I wish I'd thought to say that to Nell. What I did do was write out for her the fourth stanza of the beautiful medieval hymn, "Light's Abode, Celestial Salem":

O how glorious and resplendent, fragile body, shalt thou be, when endued with heavenly beauty, full of health and strong and free, full of vigor, full or pleasure, that shall last eternally.

—Hymn 621

Words of wonderful comfort.

I wish I'd thought to tell Nell about this transfiguration Gospel. I wish I'd thought to tell lots of people about it, myself included.

— To those whose bodies have been ravaged by disease;

— To those whose bodies have been crippled by accidents;

— To those who live each day with pain as their closest companion;

— To those now old who resent the depredations and limitations the passage of time has wrought in them;

— To those yet young who, due to the simple misfortune of growing up unattractive, live grim lives of repeated rejection.

To them all, us all: "O how glorious and resplendent, fragile body shalt thou be."

The portrait of Jesus transfigured is not just the portrait of Jesus as he shall be; it is also the portrait of us, as we shall be when we are "changed into his likeness from glory to glory" when "death is swallowed up in victory." The victory he now turns towards Jerusalem to secure there for us.

I don't know, dearest Nell, whether your little girls will recognize you in heaven or not. But I am very sure that if they do, the mother they see will be young and beautiful once more.

AMEN.

The Rev. Edward Garrigan

Spiritual Geography and the Vertigo of Grace

"Woman, believe me,
the hour is coming
when you will worship the Father
neither on this mountain nor in Jerusalem . . . "

No; we really can't start there, can we?
To launch a sermon from that line just won't work.
It would be like starting to read a short story on the
    middle of page three.

"Woman, believe me . . . "

Ripped out of context, these words make Jesus
    sound
        like one of those pious pompous pontificators
        that give preaching such a bad name.

        "The hour is coming
        when you will worship the Father
        neither on this mountain nor in Jerusalem . . . "

No, this is not, in fact, one of those bland religious
    abstractions that make so many sermons so
    unappetizing and so irrelevant.
The words of Jesus are a compassionate response to
    a burning question.

"Our ancestors worshiped on this mountain,"
   says the woman of Samaria, standing at the well,
      "but you say that the place where people
      must worship is in Jerusalem."

That doesn't sound much like a question, does it?
Sounds more like a flat assertion—a defiant challenge—like the opening gambit
      in an endless, turgid theological debate.

But listen again:
"We have worshiped on this mountain for generations"—the woman says;
      "and you people want to tell us it's the *wrong*
      place to *pray*?"

I suspect that what we are hearing
   is a question—
      an agonizing question about *spiritual
      geography*.

Spiritual geography.
That, I think, is at the core of a serious struggle
   that all but overwhelms many who make their
   way to seminary.
Folks come to seminary, at significant personal
   sacrifice,
      because they have, as the saying goes, "heard
      a call."
They come from a *familiar* and a *particular* place.
They come with a clear sense of direction.
And one day they wake up with the eerie feeling
   that they have lost their bearings;
   that they don't know where they are;
   that they are in exile on a most unfamiliar
      mountain.

Let's not worry about whose fault this is,
>or even if *anybody* is to blame.
How much good does it do, after all,
>to play the game of "pin the tail on the respon-
>sible donkey,"
>>when the road runs out, the gas gauge reads
>>empty,
>>>and the whole busload of you are stuck in
>>>the middle of nowhere?

The simple fact of the matter is,
>seminary is spiritually disorienting for lots of
>people.
They know where God has always met them before.
They know where to worship.
They have a kinesthetic personal sense of liturgical
>East.
And then the compass goes haywire.

Seminary life is by no means the only place where
>people lose their bearings.
We sometimes angrily dismiss resistance to inclusive
>language as a rationalization for misogyny.
I suspect that it *is*, in some cases.
I also suspect, however, that resistance to inclusive
>language is often a deeply felt expression of
>profound disorientation
>>when significant internal signposts seem to be
>>snatched away.

Spiritual geography, it seems to me,
>has much less to do with theological maps and
>charts,
>>than it has to do with a strongly felt sense of
>>center and balance.

"Our ancestors worshiped on *this* mountain.
How does one even begin to imagine
  what it would mean to worship anywhere else?"
I have heard sermons on the Samaritan woman
  that treat her question about worship space
    as though it were a disingenuous dodge.

Jesus is bearing down on the woman's wicked ways,
  the argument runs,
    so she tries to distract him with questions of
    liturgical trivia.
But Jesus clearly, firmly,
  brings her back to task—
  back to the painful requirement
    of facing her own personal guilt.

Perhaps.
But I wonder if that doesn't relegate the meaning
  of "repentance" to something like "moral
  re-armament."
Now, there's nothing wrong with trying to hitch up
  your moral socks.
But that's a rather superficial understanding of
  spiritual redirection; is it not?

Let's try a different read of Jesus' words at the well:

"Woman, I know how difficult this must be to grab
  hold of, but try to trust me on this if you possibly
  can:
The hour is coming when you will worship the Father
  neither on this mountain
  nor in Jerusalem.
The hour is coming, in fact, it's here already,
  when true worshipers will worship God—in spirit
  and truth."

At first hearing, this sounds downright cruel.
How disorienting can you get?
If Jesus had simply said: "Lady, you are religiously
    turned around.
        You are heading *west;* you should be going
        east.
        Go back five hundred miles to where you took the
        left fork,
            and take the *right* fork instead"—
If Jesus had simply issued the woman a fresh set of
    worship directions, then she could have said:
        "Oh, I see—thank you very much."
            or
        "I think you are mistaken.
        I'm going to stick with the map I've got."

But no. Jesus doesn't simply give the woman
    a set of directions for an alternative route.
He says something much more confusing:
"Woman," he says, "some religious signposts *are*
    clearer than others;
        but *none* of them will get you to God.
At the end of the day,
    it is inconsequential which compass azimuth you
    follow across the plane of your existence.
Because, you see, the longing love of the God who
    made you encompasses you like a sphere.

God can find you, no matter which direction you are
    going in.
But you'll do a better job of getting your own bear-
    ings, by opening yourself to an entirely new
    dimension—
        even though that will surely feel like sheer
        vertigo."

And you know what?
She gets it.
The woman really gets it.

I'm sure of that, because she doesn't say:
    "I am so sorry about my four previous husbands
    and the guy I'm currently living with."
She doesn't say:
    "Tell me what new prayers to pray, and I will pray
    them right away."
Instead, when Jesus shows her,
    not just *where she* is, but *who he is;*
        she is off like a shot—
            back home to gather the inhabitants of
            Sychar, to gather them into a joyful
            celebration,
                a celebration of how deeply they are
                grounded as a community in the
                all-knowing love of God.

The text of John's Gospel, incidentally,
    does not record the collects or the rubrics
        that this recentered community employs in
        its liturgical celebration.

Now it would be very easy at this point to sail off into
    a "risk,-uncertainty,-and-disorientation-are-
    tough-to-handle-but-good-for-you" kind of
    homily.
But that would be moralistic psychologizing,
    not a proclamation of the gospel.

Where does Jesus meet the woman of Samaria?
On "this mountain"—
    the mountain where she is already worshiping.

Jesus meets the woman at Sychar—
    the city of Jacob's well.
And this meeting is not a chance encounter.
The Gospel of John, chapter four, verse three:

> "Jesus left Judea and started back to Galilee.
> But *he had to go* through Samaria."

Peter employs an analogous evangelism strategy,
    doesn't he?
His Pentecost sermon travels through all sorts of
    places
        that are very familiar to his listeners.
Peter painstakingly preaches his way across Psalms
    and prophets.

But the track, the overarching telos of his sermon
is as plain as it can be:
    1) *Orient* the worshiping community in the
        context of its tradition.
    2) *Disorient* the worshiping community
        by *challenging the boundaries* of the tradition.
    3) *Reorient* the worshiping community
        to the *multidirectional mystery*
        of resurrection life in Jesus Christ.

The First Book of Common Prayer.
Makes a lot of difference how we celebrate this day.
The First Book, and every subsequent book, has
    provided a markpoint of theological,
    ecclesiological, and liturgical orientation.
If the direction that our heritage provides, however,
    is merely a linear one—regardless of which degree
    on the compass we follow,

it will only be one more projected escape route
from spiritual disorientation.
And ultimately, that will be just about as efficacious
as a series of road signs are in the middle of an
earthquake.

I suspect the woman of Samaria underwent an
earthquake.
I suspect that those who heard Peter preach were
similarly upended.

For, like our hearing of the Samaritan woman's story
this morning,
our hearing of Peter's Pentecost sermon also
began in the middle on page three.

"Repent and be baptized, every one of you," Peter says.
But this is not an abstract homiletical imperative
Peter is pushing.
This is not a crude, single word placard
Peter is carrying up and down the street,
wearing weird clothes on his body,
a wild look on his face,
and shaking his finger at
"To Whom It May Concern."

Peter is not doing that kind of "evangelism."
What is he doing instead?

Acts, chapter 2, verse 37:

"Now when the people heard Peter's proclamation, they were cut to the heart
and said to Peter and the other apostles,
'Brothers, what should we do?'"

And Peter said to them,
> "Repent—reorient—and be baptized every one
> of you in the name of Jesus Christ
>> so that your sins may be forgiven
>> and you will receive the gift of the Holy
>> Spirit.
> For the promise is for you, and your children,
> and for all who are far away—all who have
> lost their bearings—everyone whom the Lord
> our God calls."

Spiritual geography—critical issue
> for everyone who preaches and everyone who
> worships—

If I am hearing Jesus correctly when he speaks to
the woman,
> the first lesson in spiritual geography is that
> religious tradition is a point of orientation.

It is not an end point.
Religious tradition is a reference point,
> a place from which God
>> commences the work of our redemptive
>> reorientation.

And if that is so,
> then our worship and our preaching are most
> securely centered when we are swept off our feet,
>> and spun into the vertigo
>>> of God's utterly encompassing love.

The Rev. David J. Schlafer

What You See Is What You Get

This is an ember day; a day when by tradition we examine the meaning of being called to ministry.

Some of us respond to that call to minister by feeling privileged. We emphasize that the word of the Lord is rare, and visions are not widespread. To hear that call is a special gift, we say; and that is true.

Others of us respond to that call by shouldering a burden of responsibility: "The crowds are harassed and helpless and the laborers are few. Here I am, for you called me. I'll do it." To hear that call is to respond to a demand, we say; and that is also true.

In all the lessons for today there is gift and obligation, the promise of one and the liability of the other. That is what ministry is about. That is how it looks. That is how it feels. We are both comforted by its gift and admonished by its burden.

How have you and I come to recognize such a strange calling, such an oddly dichotomous task, feeling and seeing first privilege and then responsibility? How do we acknowledge this dual reality of the holy and the human within ourselves?

All too often we stagger under the weight of human duty, putting too much emphasis on the accountability dimension of ministry, forgetting that we are called to seek grace, not just hired to be responsible. Dick Ullman describes our vocation this way:

> It is important to be clear from the outset that [ministry], Choosing to Serve *is about a* calling

process. It is similar to a hiring process, but it is useful to compare the different features of each. Hiring *assumes an employer-employee relationship. Duties, responsibilities and power are sharply defined. Hiring is a focused decision that is in principle easily reversible. The reverse of hiring is firing.*

Calling *assumes a* community *of relationships. Sharp definitions of duties, responsibilities and power prove elusive. Calling is generally experienced as something that grows in a continuing way. The reverse of calling is dissolution.*[1]

Whether lay or ordained, those times in life when we are in greatest danger of misunderstanding ministry are when we confuse calling with hiring; and it is a confusion that arises from an overemphasis on the accountability side of the privilege and responsibility equation. Ministry is a calling. It is not a job for which one is hired. Nor is ministry therapy. We are called not to serve our own or even others' needs. We are called to serve a kingdom of grace.

A recent graduate of one of our Episcopal seminaries was interviewed for an assistant's position in a nearby parish. Questions about duties, responsibilities and power were high on his list of concerns. The job he was looking for would have a 40-hour work week and few night or weekend meetings, in order to accommodate his family's needs. But it was the final stipulation that convinced the rector this seminarian was not "called" to their parish: He refused to do weddings. This

---

[1]Richard L. Ullman, *Choosing to Serve: Resources for the Calling Process* (1991).

episode is real. It was reported to our Dean by the rector in question, a VTS alumnus. It is an example of the extent to which the concept of professionalism has overtaken vocation. It is not for nothing that the word "clergy" comes from the Greek, meaning "inheritance"; for the only inheritance of the Levites was the Lord. Ministry is a calling through which laity and ordained envision the coming of the kingdom, both feeling and seeing our way into its reality.

"OK, OK," you may respond, "So I let go of my need to cover all the bases and try to balance accountability with grace, the vision thing. How do I know when I've got the picture? How do I recognize it when I see it?" "Speak, Lord, for your servant is listening," is our plea. If the author of 1 Samuel were writing in 20th century verbiage, he would probably not write "The word of the Lord was revealed," but put something like these words in the Lord's mouth: "What you see is what you get."

That phrase is so familiar it's hard to remember when we first heard it; but these are the words of that eminent philosopher Flip Wilson. Yes, it was he who first coined the phrase, "What you see is what you get."

The same sentiment has been expressed in a more poignant way by John Cheever in his short story "Goodbye My Brother." In something like a lament he wrote, "Oh, what can you do with a man like that? What can you do? How can you dissuade his eye in a crowd from seeking out the cheek with acne, the infirm hand; how can you teach him to respond to the inestimable greatness of the race, the harsh surface beauty of life; how can you put his finger for him on the obdurate truths before which fear and horror are powerless?"

What Cheever meant and what Flip Wilson made slang is that we see what we are prepared to see: If we search for acne in a crowd, we'll find it. We see what we choose to see: If we choose to seek beauty, it is beauty we will find. In other words, we see selectively; and what we see . . . is what we get.

When Houdini, the great magician, was a small boy, his father trained him to see things other people fail to observe. Whenever they passed a store window, his father would ask him to notice the things on display just for a few seconds. After they walked on, Houdini was then asked to name the contents of the window. At first he could remember only a few items. But with practice, he learned to notice the contents of a crowded display window as he walked by and to give an accurate description of them afterward. He learned to notice as well as to see widely.

The ancient Greeks sought breadth of vision in the art of rhetoric. Rhetoric, as they envisioned it, meant the discovery of every available argument that could be brought to bear on a subject, the surfacing of difficulties on both sides of an issue in order that people might more effectively choose between conflicting opinions. For the Greeks had discovered that freedom of speech is crucial to a democracy because open dialogue is a principal method of attaining truth, particularly a method of attaining moral truth. And moral truth was what they wanted. So they discussed and debated expansively; for they knew, "What you see is what you get."

The links in the moral chain from the ancient Greeks to this century have often been broken by those who chose to see too narrowly. We need only look around us for illustrations of that point. The last few months have been full of examples:

For instance, when our election day arrived in November, this nation breathed a sigh of relief. Even if all the people you or I support are not elected, the average citizen is just plain glad when political campaigns are over. For what we are seeing and what we are getting we do not much care for. Issues are not debated because it is not at issues that most of the candidates are looking: Many see only the negatives in their opponents; so it is negatives that we get. Few and far between are the candidates who choose to seek Cheever's obdurate truths; so few and far between are the truths that are being found.

In introducing a collection of his stories, Cheever once described the "constants that I look for": a "love of light and a determination to trace some moral chain of being." The only constant apparent in our elections is a desire to win. No moral chain of being is uncovered because no one running and no one watching is apparently looking for such a chain. A community in conversation about the truth is lacking.

What does that say about us as a nation, and what are the ramifications for those of us who call ourselves Christians? You and I are not Christians simply because God has promised us good times in the sky by and by. No, we are Christians because we have chosen to honor something of value: the gift of grace. Are we not, then, uniquely responsible for the obdurate truths before which fear and horror are powerless? Have we not been gifted in this world with the ability to see the greatness of humanity and seek it? Are not the graced particularly responsible to make a moral difference?

In the foreword to a book entitled *Orators and Philosophers, a history of the idea of Liberal Education,* Joseph Featherstone writes, "The educated man or woman must know philosophy and express it effectively to an audience. The educated person must know how to create a community of hearers. Learning has to make a moral difference, and the circle of moral speech and concern is what the philosophers neglect to the peril of their souls."

In other words, the educated man or woman learns from history and tradition and with reason puts that knowledge to work to change the world for the better. Our health, our ability to relate to others, our future success depend on what we see. If we see more good than bad, more positive than negative, good is what we will get. Those who expect the future to be better than the past are generally right; for studies have confirmed that people who see themselves as winners, even in difficult times, usually are. And it is more than "the power of positive thinking." It is a way of looking at the breadth of our opportunities. For what you see is what you get.

Football coaches understand this adage well. As we approach the season of football frenzy, I am reminded of Coach John Madden's example of the effect of perception on performance in his book *Knee*. He tells about Ray Wersching, kicker for the San Francisco 49'ers. It seems that Wersching didn't even look at the goalposts when he lined up for a field goal. In fact he never looked at the goalposts. The quarterback had to tell him if a kick were successful.

"But how do you aim," Madden once asked him, "if you don't look at the goalposts?"

"I just look at the hash marks," said Wersching. "They tell me all I have to know."

Madden went on to note that Wersching was right. The hash marks, those chalked lines about 23 yards inside each sideline on a football field were then $18 \frac{1}{2}$ feet apart, the same width as the goalposts. In a sense, the goalposts came up out of the hash marks.

"The farther away you are, the narrower the goalposts look," explained Ray Wersching. "But the hash marks always look wide."

Ray Wersching brought to his challenges breadth of vision, the vision thing. And seeing more, he got more.

The wider your field of vision, the better your chances. You know from your own experience, the broader your field of knowledge, the more you get out of every opportunity. The more you bring to a situation, the more you gain from it. If you play a musical instrument, when you attend a concert the experience is richer for you than for the person who knows nothing about music. You can follow the part of the instrument you play and bask in the fullness of its blending with the other instruments.

Or take the experience of visiting an art museum. There is much to see in simply strolling through the galleries, but how much more satisfying to rent an audio-tape and learn what to look for. You see more deeply and get much more.

It is simply a matter of fact that the more you know, the more you get out of life. The more you know, the more choices you have. The broader your vision, the greater your opportunities; for what you see is what you get.

Look and listen, then, for the holy juxtaposed alongside the human, for stepping stones rather than stumbling blocks to your calling. Build upon a vision of holiness, always ready for the gifts of God. Make a space in your life for the grace of God, and you shall get all the truth and beauty life can hold. Expect it, and you will find it.

The Rev. Judith McDaniel

Sacraments and Sacred Metaphors

One of the commitments that has always characterized Anglican worship is the clear conviction that "body language" is as important as the language of a written/spoken text. Proclamation of the gospel requires more than a "talking head." Every one of the seven sacraments recognized by Episcopal Christians is, literally, a *tangible* manifestation of God's grace. Through the touch of a designated minister—not necessarily an ordained one—through direct physical contact, or through the intentional, "careful" administration of water, wine, bread, or oil, God's love is proclaimed in ways that words alone can neither replicate nor stand in for as a substitute.

Sometimes, unfortunately, preachers feel that they have to use sermon words to explain or extensively refer to the sacramental dimension of gospel proclamation. It is almost as though they feel required to use words as neon arrows, flashing toward Baptism, Eucharist, ordination, or healing unction; just to make sure that those who participate in the sacraments will "get the point."

The effect, of course, is not unlike what happens when a would-be comedian tries to "explain a joke." If the joke is well told, it needs no explanation; if it is poorly told, no explanation will help.

It does not follow from this, however, that preaching (in the more restricted sense of the word) should operate independently of sacramental proclamation—one hand not taking account of what the other hand is doing. It is possible and necessary to complement the tangible Word with a spoken one. The sermons in the following section are clear examples of how the sacraments can be embellished by "grace notes."

The first sermon in this section was preached in a university chapel context, where the baptism of a child of faculty parents brought to the service many unchurched and religiously skeptical colleagues of those parents (who were highly respected in the academic community). **Robert Hirschfield,** the vicar-chaplain explicitly chooses not to use the setting as an occasion for a conceptual apologetic defense of the ancient ritual. Instead, he takes a sermon tack more akin to Jesus' frequent response to hostile analytical challengers—he approaches their questions by way of image, symbol, and implied story. Hirschfield invites his listeners into the experience of baptismal history, rather than trying to give them an abstract justification of it.

Preached in a more "parish family" context, **Glenn Busch** also intends, by way of multi-sensory imagination, to help his community, who gather weekly for the Eucharist, to taste the power of table fellowship at the Messianic Banquet "again for the first time." The way of images, in other words, is often as necessary for the faithful as it is for the skeptical.

The next two sermons make more use of argument. **Roger Alling** persuasively evokes the sense of rational and spiritual irresponsibility implicit in the Episcopal Church's current downsizing of commitment to ministry and to seminary preaching instruction. A time of declining church participation, he argues forcefully, is precisely the time for a firmer, more faithful commitment of resources.

Karen Siegfriedt is even more explicitly didactic (clearly demonstrating that such a sermon strategy need not be dull, lifeless, or abstract), using the preaching moment as the occasion for solid teaching on a troublesome text from Ephesians, and an agonizing contemporary social dilemma. This is solid, straightforward talk about the sacrament of marriage, in a setting where stories and picture language would have far less lasting significance.

Barbara Crafton touches our hearts at their tenderest places, when by means of an artistic and theologically sensitive rendering of a live parish situation, she brings us powerfully and deeply into the experience of what it means to experience the sacrament of healing.

Jennifer Phillips moves back toward the left side of the brain. She begins with a splendid, tangible metaphor of "blessing," and leads her congregation in a searching analysis of what is going on every time we receive and offer the power of God's sacramental gift of saving life.

Each of these sermons is an illustration of preaching as it is defined in the title of a book by retired Archbishop of Canterbury Donald Coggan: *Preaching: The Sacrament of the Word.* Just as Baptism, Eucharist, ordination, marriage, and healing interweave in meaning with each other, and all point toward "Christ, the Sacrament of God," so preaching that is sacramentally sensitive (as opposed to sacramentally explanatory) is enhanced, and enhances the other sacramental dimensions of God's tangible, graceful action in the church.

Baptism of Benjamin John Hiskes

This Is the Water

This is the water on which God breathed and the Spirit brooded when God began creating us . . . all creeping things, all races, male and female.

This is the water that drove up the trunk of the tree whose branches bore the fruit we weren't to taste.

This water covered the earth deeper than the Himalayas when God wanted to start over.

This is the foot of the rainbow that's meant to tell us God won't destroy the creation again.

This is the place where Abraham let down his son Isaac, and the place where the ram came at the last minute to rescue all us parents who inevitably fail our children.

This is the water of the River Jabbock where Jacob still wrestles with God.

This is the well where Joseph was left for dead by his jealous brothers.

This is the water that opened at Moses' command when God led his people out of slavery. This is the water that clogged the wheels of Pharoah's army and then swallowed them whole.

This water sprung from rocks in the desert when the people started whining to go back to the way things used to be.

This water was lapped up by the tongues of fire when Elijah went head to head against the prophets of Baal.

In this water Elisha made an ax head float.

This is the water that Bathsheeba used to bathe in when David saw her from his roof-top.

These are the salty tears King David shed when Nathan accused him of the worst sin. These are the tears he shed when he pleaded God for forgiveness, and got it.

These are the waters of Babylon by which our ancestors sat down and wept, their harps and tongues silent for homesickness.

This is the water that Ezekiel saw flood the temple, washing away all rank churchy-ness and filling the whole world with living trees that feed and heal.

And this is the water that broke in a barn in Bethlehem.

Out of this water John pulled a stunned Jesus in the River Jordan, the day they saw the dove and heard from deep within the Voice that said, "YOU ARE MY BELOVED. IN YOU MY HEART SINGS FOR JOY!"

This is where those men heaved and hauled nets, until love came to town and called them to even harder work for even less pay.

This is the water that became wine at a wedding in Cana.

Peter sauntered on this water, and then sank, and then was rescued, setting the pattern of a disciple's life.

This is the well in Samaria where Jesus chatted, unchaperoned, with a disreputable woman. This is the living water that quenched her thirst forever, and restored her dignity.

This is the spittle that came from his mouth when he made the deaf hear and the blind see.

This is the water he used to cut the wine at his last meal.

These are the tears that fell that last night in the garden.

This is the sink that Pilate used to wash his hands when he passed the death sentence.

This is what he thirsted for at the hour of his death, and this is what flowed out of his side, out of the wound in which we seek to hide from the evil one.

This is the stone rolled away from the cave where he was lain.

This is the tomb from which he blasted . . . this is the opening, this is the way.

This is the water he gives to bind us to him when he destroys shame and sin and death . . . This is the water that tells us who we are, and whose we are.

This is our restored memory, our freedom, our light and life.

What event in our lives, what triumph or failure, what joy or sadness, can't be linked, plunged into the story that adopts us, and adopts Benjamin this morning?

This is water. It comes from the deep in the ground and then out of a tap, the faucet in the other room. But this morning our prayers and the prayers of Jesus engage the Holy Spirit and so we believe this water comes from the deepest heart of the Trinity. This morning this water scoops Benjamin up, and all of us with this lovely child, into the life of the Eternal. For this morning God bestows his whole story of salvation on Benjamin, who today is crowned a saint, a brother of Jesus. Forever and ever. AMEN.

The Rev. A. Robert Hirschfeld

A Tale of Two Tables

Here begins a tale of two tables. The first is my grandmother's table. How I loved to slide my legs under those worn rectangular planks, all wide-eyed and ready. I can still put it away, and I had my early training around Maggie Forse's table. She was an accomplished and consummate cook.

Glistening golden noodles, awash in butter and flaked with parsley, appealed as much to the eye as to the palate. Mashed potatoes, the steam curling around the bowl like fog on a miniature mound of snow. Gravy so thick it eased heavy from the ladle; gravy made from the juice of a tender roast that cooked for hours in a long, slow oven. Homemade biscuits, and a kaleidoscope of vegetables in bright and varied colors. How I wish we still had her recipe for turkey stuffing: spices, herbs and bread, all playing the right notes in that rich symphony of ingredients.

I don't just see that table in my mind's eye, I can smell it. I can feel my hands resting on the hard, flat surface with the white linen cloth. And I can still taste those noodles as if I had eaten them for lunch.

It was an event, not just a meal, to slide your chair up to Maggie's table. And Thanksgiving . . . well, that was her tour de force. It was the annual culinary extravaganza, a dazzling array of food and drink, a crowded table of gastronomical excellence that mocks my mere words of description. That woman could cook. She had no challengers.

I have a lot of memories around my grandmother's table, just as you have memories around the tables of your life and times. Tables are often the places where memories are made. Tables connect us with our past; around them we gather to remember; to make and renew friendships; and to connect with our heritage. And, sometimes, we connect with something deeper . . . something that connects us with life itself.

The symbol for Thanksgiving might better be the table than the turkey. Most of us do make an effort to get back to our roots, to pull up to the table with those we love, for Thanksgiving.

There is something powerful about tables that touches us deep within. Even when we are not always sure what is drawing us to the table, we feel that inexorable pull.

Thanksgiving will be around our table this year. My grandmother has been dead for years; the family has changed; and, alas, with aging parents and growing children still too young to have their own homes, ours is now the place to come home to. We have assumed that position. So I will light the fire, and we will sit by it, like our prehistoric forebears who huddled around their fires for warmth and protection, and no doubt connected with their past as they pondered an uncertain future. And, of course, the table will be there.

Every family should have a special table, one they keep going back to, one that reminds them of who they are, where they have come from, and what they value; a table where they come to be fed, comforted and loved.

Tables are powerful places. Last year while our family was visiting prospective colleges, we made a trip to Philadelphia where we toured Constitution Hall. There I stood not twenty feet from the table where Benjamin Franklin sat. I saw the table where the

Declaration of Independence was signed. I was moved by that. So much of importance happens around the table. "Come over, let's have dinner." "Mr. Rabin and Mr. Arafat, please sit here at the table while you sign these peace accords." "Let's get the cards on the table." "Labor and management sat down at the negotiating table to work on an agreement." Wasn't it the lunch counter that became the symbol, the central figure in the early days of desegregation?

Never underestimate the power of the table around which you gather. Mighty things take place there, experiences that may affect you for the rest of your life, even when you have no notion of their taking place. That is the way of tables.

This Thanksgiving I get to preside at two tables. Remember, there is another table in this tale.

I am so glad that we have moved the second table out, away from the wall. When the family gathers we should face one another. No one should have his back turned on the rest of the family. Everyone has a place. All are welcome; none are turned away.

We have already lighted the fire. Soon I will set the table with pieces of bread and blood-red wine. And won't we have some memories to recall: "Whenever you drink it, do this for the remembrance of me." "We celebrate the memorial of our redemption, O Father, in this sacrifice of praise and thanksgiving." Eucharist comes from a Greek word that means simply: Thanksgiving. This, too, is a Thanksgiving table.

The two tables run together in my vision, both helping me to be more grateful for my life and all my experiences.

The Anglican poet, George Herbert, whose 400th birthday we celebrated last year, made this poetic expression: "Thou that has given so much to me, give one thing more—a grateful heart." These two tables preserve the memories of much for which to be thankful.

Sometimes I fear that it is hard to have a grateful heart in our land today. We are becoming a nation of complainers—"Give me," "You owe me"—more concerned about blaming and finding fault than accepting responsibility and finding solutions. More full of resentment than gratitude. The only cure for all of that is a grateful heart, and a humble sense of thanksgiving.

It is so important that we return to the table and be grateful . . . grateful for the greatest gift of all. "This is my body, which is given for you. Do this for the remembrance of me." Soul food, food that gives us the energy to keep plugging along, to slide back from the table and walk back out the door into an ungrateful world—a world that just might be improved by the presence of a few more grateful hearts.

Come on now, the table is about to be set. Let us gather around. Let us eat, drink, be joyful and make Thanksgiving for all the memories that give us life . . . real life.

The Rev. Glenn E. Busch

Mission Attrition

Proper: Numbers 11:16-17; 24-29
          St. John 4:31-38

There aren't as many people teaching preaching at Episcopal seminaries today as there were a few years ago. It's the same old story . . . budget constraints and the need to downsize and cut staffs.

Seminary enrollments are down also. "Why is that?", I asked in a recent conversation with one of the seminary deans. He said "The seminaries reflect what is going on in the wider church. Fewer and fewer people are being accepted for ordination by the dioceses. There aren't as many full-time church jobs."

Why accept candidates, put them through the expense and the effort to receive training and then be unable to employ them when all of that is through? What shall we do about the ordained ministry?

Eldad and Medad never went to the Tent of Meeting with the other seventy Elders. They weren't present when God shared the Spirit with the seventy so that Moses would be able to bear the burden and accomplish his mission. They prophesied anyway and as they did so, they were observed by one of Moses' young assistants. It has been suggested that this young assistant might have been Joshua.

No irregular prophesying for Joshua! Perhaps he was the chairman of the Commission on Ministry. Now Joshua knew a wall when he saw one. Jericho's might have to come down but he's ready to raise one now to keep Eldad and Medad out of the prophesying business. Joshua got nowhere with the boss. Moses was delighted at the news about Eldad and Medad. He said, "Would that all God's people were prophets."

We must be getting toward the end of our church's Decade of Evangelism, which a cynical friend of mine calls the "Decade of talking about evangelism." A month ago the New York Times published a five-part series on the new mega-churches that are growing by leaps and bounds. What the Times had to say about us, and churches like us, is that we are decreasing in numerical strength while the mega-churches are growing. Do we ever ask why?

I can't but wonder whether we ever make the connection between the diminishing of church jobs, the loss of full-time preaching positions in our seminaries, the "guard the entrances mentality" of so many of our Commissions on Ministry with our lackluster evangelism. Why would we adopt "mission attrition" as a strategy to deal with our decline in numbers and finances? Where is the theology in that? Where is the common sense? How can you argue that you need fewer clergy, fewer preachers, fewer churches and fewer professors of preaching in a time of ecclesiastical decline?

We need more vocations, more churches, more good preaching and more good preaching instruction if we are to have any hope at all in arresting our decline, guarding and preserving our tradition, and contributing the rich body of Anglican Christianity to future generations. I shudder when I think of how thankless we are towards those who came before us. Our Anglican predecessors struggled against their own obstacles so that we might have the rich household of faith and practice that we cherish. How in good conscience can we do less?

Today is an Ember Day. An Ember Day is a good time to pray for the ministry and for those who present themselves for ordained ministry. Ministry is a vocation. To be a minister is also a job of work, a way to make a living. The fourth chapter of St. John's Gospel talks about these two realities.

Making a living is sometimes described as putting bread on the table. On that hot day in Sychar of Samaria, getting the evening meal is on the disciples mind so they go to town to get provisions. While they're gone, Jesus encounters the Samaritan woman at Jacob's well and they have a rich conversation about drink. Later the disciples return and encourage Jesus to eat. Jesus responds with what is on his mind and it is clearly food of a different sort. He says, "My food is to do the will of him who sent me and to complete his work."

Now food doesn't just come out of nowhere, so the conversation turns next to the harvest, but not a harvest of corn or grain. This harvest is a harvest of people and of souls. It is a gathering of the people who are responding to the good news of the Kingdom, the preaching of the gospel. Look around you, Jesus says. The fields are ripe for harvest. The sower and the reaper will rejoice together.

Now there was an old saying about sowing and reaping which was sad and pessimistic. It went like this. "One sows and another reaps." Woe is me! I worked and someone else will get the benefit. Life is unfair.

Do you see what Jesus has done with this old idea? What Jesus says is that there is so much abundance, so much potential for growth, so much to be gathered in that the sower and reaper work in tandem. No need to wait for crops to grow; their abundance is immediate. Life in the kingdom is not unfair and scarcity has been done away. The fields are rich. Harvesting should be going on all the time.

If you and I are going to be evangelists today there are some things we will have to think about again. We need to think about the very nature of evangelism itself.

Evangelism is proclaiming the gospel to people who haven't heard it yet or who have heard it and forgotten it. This means talking to people who are outside of the church.

Do we have a strategy for communicating the gospel to non-church people today? Is preaching a part of that strategy? Is preaching the only part?

In a recent newsletter, Martin Marty quotes William Miehl, a recently retired professor of preaching in one of our seminaries, to the point that most preachers fail to account for how many of their hearers on a Sunday morning almost didn't come to church that day, are not at all sure of what they believe or even why they're there.

I wonder if we think about that while we are preparing to preach? Are we ready to address the people in our pews who almost didn't come that morning?

If we are to be practical about Miehl's idea we will have to assume that at least some of our congregation needs to be evangelized. If we remember this we will approach the texts in a very different way. Those who are already believers may want us to put exclamation marks around the text. Others may need us to speak to the question marks raised for them by the readings.

Preaching is part of our evangelistic strategy, but not the only part. For the most part, preaching is clergy work. Crucial to the evangelism task is raising up the laity for ministry.

We must not, as ordained persons in the church, believe the falsehood that evangelism is all up to us.

It is the laity who are in daily contact with people in the world who have either never heard the word of the gospel or who have since forgotten it. Our job is to inspire them to share their faith and train them in the skills they need. I have met many men and women in my life who are ready and eager to do this work and only wait to be asked to do so by the leaders of their churches and helped in the skills they need for the job.

I earnestly pray that we can lay aside our defeatist mentality. I hope that we can return to praying for vocations rather than worrying about placing people in ecclesiastical slots. I hope that dioceses will regain their missionary fervor and never close a church in their jurisdiction before they have labored to form a new congregation to take up the task of witness and proclamation. I hope that seminary boards will insist that all of their students graduate with every degree of preaching excellence obtainable and insist that every opportunity for help in this field be offered to each of their students.

"But I tell you, look around you, and see how the fields are ripe for harvesting." We have every reason in the world to believe this word of Jesus. The time between sowing and reaping is short and we need not wait for a new day or another time.

Like Jesus, our food should be to do the will of him who sent us and to share in the completion of his work. Why not pray with that intention each time we ask for daily bread?

The Rev. Roger Alling

Christian Marriage Re-examined

Wives be subject to your husbands as you are to the Lord. I'll bet you never thought I would begin a sermon with this quotation from the Letter to the Ephesians. After all, would not any independent female balk at the notion of being subject to her husband? Today's reading from Ephesians is one of the passages from scripture that the prayer book suggests to be read at a wedding. Yet in my limited experience as a priest, I have never presided over a wedding, nor attended one, at which this passage was read. Why do you think that is? Do you think that this passage has been misinterpreted by some husbands as the right to dominate or abuse their wives? Do you think that this passage has been used to coerce women into staying in relationships that are harmful and ultimately destructive?

I think scripture has been misused in many ways. This is a shame. Passages like today's reading have been taken out of the context in which they were written and have been used as power plays. But when we know in our hearts that the message of God in Christ has to do with universal servanthood, inclusivity, peace, justice, and love, we can approach scripture with a sincere desire to grow in the likeness of Christ. Then we do not have to be afraid of passages like these. The Holy One whom we adore longs for our wholeness and happiness. Abuse, neglect, and power plays are not part of God's vocabulary. They are only part of God's tears.

What I would like to talk about today is a Christian way of relating to each other that seems foreign to today's culture. In particular, I would like to talk about marriage. The words that I say today would also apply to anyone who is in a long term committed relationship, or even those of us who are single but long to mature into the full stature of Christ. The Epistle to the Ephesians is not a marriage manual. It is rather a letter sent to many churches around the year 100 A.D. It explains to the churches that the ultimate unity of all people and all things can only be found in Jesus Christ. It reminds the people that the purpose of the church is to be God's instrument of reconciliation. Some commentators would say that the Letter to the Ephesians is "the highest reach of New Testament thought." Let us enter into that highest reach of New Testament thought and try to understand what God might be saying to us.

Wives, be subject to your husbands. I recently read that 50 percent of all marriages in the United States end in divorce and that about 50 percent of all married people commit adultery. There are literally hundreds of books out there to help couples save their marriages. Psychologists and therapists are working overtime helping couples improve their relationships. There are courses, seminars, and retreats—all of which attempt to support and give insight into healthy marriages. And yet, the rate of divorce is at an all-time high. The state of marriage has become for most a very tenuous proposition. Why is this?

At no time in history have the expectations of a spouse been so great as they are today. No wonder marriages are in such a ragged state. In the ancient Greco-Roman world, this is what it meant to be married: "To have sons one can introduce to the family and the neighbors, and to have daughters of one's own to give to husbands. For we have courtesans for pleasure, concubines to attend to our daily bodily needs, and wives to bear children legitimately and to be faithful wards of our homes." It is only in recent western culture that love has been a primary concern in a marriage. Most marriages throughout history have been arranged. Emotional and sexual aspects of the marriage were secondary. It was only hoped that love would follow marriage.

In the Hebrew Scriptures marriage was motivated by the command to be fruitful and multiply. Women and children were the property of the patriarch of the house to be used by the man. A wife held no status in the family until she bore sons. Sterile women who could not produce an heir often gave their maids to their husbands for that purpose. As you recall, Sarah gave her maid to Abraham when she could not produce a son. Love, encouragement, mutual satisfaction, and understanding were not the grounds for choosing a marriage partner. In those days, matrimony had more to do with business deals concerning dynastic and property considerations. In order to save his life from the Egyptians and again from Abimelech, Abraham, our great forefather, allowed his wife to be taken away and used by Pharaoh and the King. In Hebrew culture, adultery was a property offense, not a moral one. We all know the story of Solomon and his 700 wives and 300 concubines.

Historically, Christianity did little to raise the consciousness regarding marriage. The church remained overwhelmingly ambivalent about most forms of marriage. This is no surprise given that Jesus did not marry, did not have a biological father, nor were his parents married at the time of his conception. In Roman Catholic circles, Jesus had no siblings either.

In the early years of the Christian Church, celibacy and virginity were valued higher than the state of marriage. Procreation was looked upon as the sole purpose of marriage. In the 4th century, St. Augustine set the theological tone based on his experience as a lustful and selfish youth. He said that "marriage is for procreation and this is good, yet procreation is impossible without lust and this is sinful." Marriage was not made a sacrament until the 13th century.

During the Protestant Reformation a new concept of family and marriage began to emerge. Luther removed marriage from the list of sacraments, revolted against the concept of celibacy, and regarded marriage as the proper forum for the expression of sexual desires. However, marriage was still driven by property and population concerns even though love began to play a minor role in the decision to get married.

For most of history marriage was a practical matter. But in this century, particularly in the latter half, marriage has taken on a new role. The population base is no longer the driving factor in getting married. According to Dr. Harville Hendrix, who wrote a best seller called *Getting the Love You Want,* people get married to further their own psychological and emotional growth. Today, people have tremendous expectations of their partners. They expect that the partner will satisfy unmet childhood needs, complement them where they are lacking, nurture them in a consistent and loving way, and be eternally available to them. Once a couple is married and the relationship seems secure, a psychological switch is triggered deep in the old brain that activates all the latent infantile wishes. It is as if the wounded child takes over and the child says, "I've been good enough long enough to ensure that this person is going to stay around for awhile. Let's see the payoff." So husbands and wives take a big step back from each other and wait for the dividends of togetherness to start to roll in.

And to make things more complicated, there are now three roles to fulfill in a marriage for most people. In the past, there were only two roles. One role was the bread winner, and the other role was the nurturer of children and the caretaker of the household. But now that both parents work, and there are only two people to fulfill those three roles, couples are stressed out, have little quality time to talk to each other, and even less time to develop rituals that, in the past, held the family together. And to think that the other person can meet all our unmet childhood needs and attend to three pragmatic or work or job roles, it is no wonder people resort to divorce.

A well known prelate recently said that matrimony has become a ragged institution in the second half of this century. What are we to do? I think that if we seek simply a functional marriage in which each partner enters into a predetermined role for the purpose of economic stability and the raising of children, then we have enough models to follow. If we follow these old models then chances are the marriage will be stable and orderly. It may not be happy, but the marriage will be predictable. But if we marry for mutual joy, and for the help and comfort given to another in prosperity and adversity, then I think we need to seek the advice of the highest reach of New Testament thought which may be found in today's reading from Ephesians.

Our reading today does not begin with *Wives, be subject to your husbands.* It begins with *be subject to one another out of reverence for Christ.* What we are talking about here is voluntary subjection, a mutual readiness to renounce one's own will for another in order to move that relationship towards wholeness. This does not mean that we allow ourselves to be abused. But there comes a time when we need to mature, and move beyond our own unmet childhood needs and become a healing presence in the world. This is where the concept of subjection fits in. But I think we can only subject ourselves to one another when our spiritual needs are addressed. Thus, the need for spiritual community and for learning how to put Christ at the center of ourselves, our souls and our bodies, is an integral part of making a marriage work.

These are not the empty words of a preacher. When we love and feel loved by the perfect lover, who is God, we can let loose of the expectation that our partner will be the perfect lover. Statistics have shown that couples who pray daily and who have warm images of God, are those who are most likely to have sexual fulfillment and good marriages.

After we hear the words *to be subject to one another,* the author of Ephesians then says, *wives be subject to your husbands,* not as society dictates, but *as to the Lord. Husbands, love your wives as Christ loved the Church.* I do not want to get into the battle of the sexes, but I think we all agree that people are different. Sometimes this means that women have different needs than men. In this example, and it is only one example, the author is saying that men tend to have issues surrounding power and it is important for women to be sensitive to those issues. Women tend to have a great need for affection and so men are called to love their wives as themselves so that this need can be met. These are only general examples. They are not the only examples. Each of us knows what the particular need is of that special person in our life. And so we are being called to move beyond our own unmet childhood needs, and really reach out and honor that need of the one to whom we are committed.

My brother, Kirk, died recently. He struggled with pneumonia for about a month. There were times when he did not appear to be trying hard enough to fight against it. He would not move enough, cough enough, or eat enough. This upset his wife very much because she was afraid that he would die and leave her alone with a four-year-old child. A few days before he died, she said to him, "Kirk, I am here to do whatever I can to help you get better. I'll make you whatever food you want, I'll sit here, I'll help you get up, whatever you want, I am here for you. But I also know that you are so tired, so tired of fighting to survive. If you want to give up, then I want you to let go. Kyra and I will be fine and so I don't want you to worry about us. I will stay with you and help you let go. Just let me know what I can do for you." My brother did not have the ideal marriage, but I do think that my sister-in-law knew what it meant to move beyond her unmet childhood needs and be subject to another.

Mutual subjection must be an integral part of today's marriages. A pagan marriage is one in which two clashing egos try to form a union in which mutual subjection, repentance, and forgiveness are unknown. A Christian marriage, on the other hand, is one of mutual submission; one in which the Holy Spirit is at the center, inspiring the couple with wisdom and devotion in the ordering of their common life, "that each may be to the other a strength in need, a counselor in perplexity, a comfort in sorrow, and a companion in joy." (Book of Common Prayer, p. 429)

The Rev. Karen F. Siegfriedt

Turning Back and Giving Praise

*Were not the ten cleansed? Where are the
nine? Was no one found to return and give
praise to God except this foreigner? And he
said to him, "Rise and go your way; your
faith has made you well."* —Luke 17:18-19

Ten are healed. One comes back to praise God. That's
about the ratio we're familiar with, isn't it? Many lives
are saved by the healing power of the Spirit of God, and
many people just keep right on going, not even realizing
what has happened to them. But for those who turn
back and give God praise, the circle of love is com-
pleted. They know who they are and they know what
God has done. They know that there really isn't anything else they *need* to know. And whatever happens to
them in the future, they do not forget whose they are.

Bill and I were walking back to my place after dinner
at Fedora, which is Bill's favorite restaurant. A bicycle
passed us swiftly, its rider high on the seat and low over
the handlebars, wearing a helmet and those black
Spandex shorts that people on bicycles wear today. "I
really miss riding a bike," Bill said, and I nodded and
said, "Yeah, I'll bet you do," as we turned up Eleventh
Street and continued our slow walk. We always walk
slowly, Bill and I, slower than I walk when I'm alone.
Because Bill's right side is paralyzed, and he wears a
heavy brace on his leg, and he holds one arm bent
against his chest so his two arms don't swing when he

walks like other people's arms do to help them along. Bill lurches from side to side when he walks—or at least, he did when he walked—but he can maintain a pretty decent clip when he gets going. Or rather, he *used* to.

I'm having a little trouble with my verb tenses, where Bill is concerned. He's lying in a hospital bed now, blood seeping into his brain from a tumor buried somewhere deep within it. His walking days are over. His talking days, too, and the writing days which took their place (a little magic slate like we had when we were kids: Bill's communications link to the world after his speech went last week). His seeing days are behind him. At thirty-five, the powers of his body are abandoning him, one by one, and his death is now very near. "I gave him the last rites yesterday," my colleague tells me on the phone, "I think he understood. I think he was making the responses, trying to make them, anyway: I mean, all he could do was groan."

We have lots of thirty-five-year olds dying at St. John's—more than I ever thought I'd see, back in the days before I knew that the remaining decades of my ministry would be filled with young people dying. But Bill isn't dying of AIDS, as all those others are. He got this brain tumor when he was fourteen—almost died then, but they pulled him through, with only the paralysis to show for a terrible year's ordeal. "That must have been tough," I said when he was telling me about it one day at the coffee shop, and he smiled. "Yeah, you see, I had just realized I was gay," he said, "and when I got sick I thought God was punishing me." I stirred my coffee and said nothing; he talked on about his Catholic upbringing and his guilt, about his self-loathing, about his terror and his pain. We talked, as we always do, about his recovery from the alcoholism and drug abuse in which he had buried that pain for a dozen years or so. We talk about what serenity means. What responsibility means. Bill's always beating himself up about his failures. I think about him struggling out of bed in the morning and strapping on his leg brace to go to work, and I tell him he sure doesn't look like a failure to me.

We talk a lot about healing. We did, I mean, when Bill could talk. Eight years of sobriety is a powerful healing. Discovering a Christian faith that isn't all about shame and guilt is another; Bill's come to know that the Higher Power that delivered him from the bondage of addiction is Jesus Christ, and I would see him at the Eucharist, or at Morning Prayer, bowing from the waist in a solemn bow at the name of Jesus, and crossing himself very slowly and deliberately. He wears a cross around his neck—sometimes two or three crosses, and sometimes he wears a cross earring on one ear, as well: Bill's quite a unique dresser. "I know that God doesn't hate me. I keep slipping into my old self-hatred," he says, "but I know that God doesn't hate me. It wasn't true that he made me sick because I was gay. That wasn't true."

"No, it wasn't," I tell him, and I feel myself shaking: I am so angry at whoever taught a young boy to believe in a God who would send him a brain tumor for being gay that I just don't trust myself to speak further. We talk about the love of God in guiding him toward sobriety and new relationships with people in AA, about the place of confession in his new life in Christ, about the presence of Christ in the body and the blood—"I stay away from the blood myself," he says, "a little too close to home, so is it really true that the bread alone is enough?" and I tell him yes, it is really true. Bill loves to talk about the ins and outs of Church tradition.

Loves trick questions. He loves to visit the monastery. He attends the inquirers' class. Last year he was received into the Episcopal Church at the Cathedral. "I don't know if my parents will come," he says, wistfully, but they did come.

"Things are about the same," says his mother now when I call the hospital. "He's not really awake at all now. They say it won't be too much longer."

The body that now lies dying knows very well what it is to live with pain and weakness. But still his faith has made him well—he groans out the responses in the church's last anointing of his body on this side of heaven, inarticulate groans that mean "And also with you" and "AMEN," as he prepares to leave his maimed physical body for his perfect spiritual one. His soul has gotten strong. His soul is what will remain. And his soul belongs to Christ, and he knows it. And it is enough. So Bill was healed—of so many things. And he was one of the ones who turned back and praised God—one of the ones you might not expect to do so, would you, because of the many ways in which he was *not* healed. That fourteen-year-old boy never rode a bike again. I think of him, the way he will be soon, and I send him this vision: *In glory, Bill: strong, both arms free and both legs pumping hard, riding a bike as fast as the wind right into the city of God.*

AMEN.

The Rev. Barbara Cawthorne Crafton

Blessing As We Are Blessed

I stood in line at the cash register in a little shop called "Good Good the Elephant" buying some cards last week, and watched as the mother of a little girl in front of me bought for her delighted child (perhaps six years old) a magic wand: one of the transparent ones filled with fluid through which sparkles and stars drift in a glitter of color. As I followed them out of the shop I watched as the little girl clutched her wand and went dancing down the sidewalk, elfin fashion, touching things with it: a flowering shrub, the pickets of a fence, the fender of a car, some overhanging branches of a birch just venturing into leaf, her mother's shoulder, the head of a passing cocker spaniel. And as she touched each thing she would laugh as they were transformed by the radiance of her expectation into things glowing and new for her . . . and it seemed, also for me.

It seemed to me that this child had captured the essence of what it is that we human beings do when we bless, as we are to do today moving around the landmarks of our city neighborhood with holy water, incense and with prayer. A spirit of gratitude and delight flowed from the child back to the invisible Provider of all delights whose laughter laughed inside her own. She saw with a child's fleeting but deep attention the things of the concrete world and their need for transformation, for that touch which would awaken the numinous glory hidden within them. She reached and touched, lovingly willing their wondrous awakening with all her energy, and believing in the power of goodness and life to accomplish that which she purposed. And then she saw transformation into being, not only as the world of her viewing sparkled into animation, but also as her own seeing was renewed and filled with wonder.

Our blessing too, crusty old grown ups as we are (most of us), is an act of praise which "recreate[s] an unblemished world" as "By referring all things back to their creator we see them again lit up by the light of [God's] . . . glory, shot through with the energies of [God's] . . . wisdom and . . . love. We see that unblemished world of origins, in which God saw all that [God]... had made, and behold it was very good."[1] And we see it in the plain, everyday, grimy, and unperfected substance of our city. Light struggles to break through the opaque surfaces and shimmers in the dance of every atom. We see it with the eyes of love, in the Spirit of the One who has first loved us, and whose compassion is over all that God has made. All of the goodness we perceive comes from God; and signals God's presence in creation, and creation's participation in God.

There are those who fear that such language smacks of pantheism, of reducing God to a sort of impersonal animating spirit contained in the universe. Such a view would be far from Christian. Our Anglican and catholic tradition, however, takes pains to clarify that Creator and creation enjoy a mutual participation and connection in which each is quite distinct, but no longer separate.[2]

---

[1] A.M.Allchin, *Praise Above All* (Caerdif: University of Wales Press, 1991), p.4.

[2] *Panentheism* is the technical term, and it is a properly Christian, catholic, and Anglican understanding of the relationship between God and creation, though not shared by all in any of those categories.

When we pray for our city, we recognize God as having an interest in it: in its commerce and learning, in its healing and housing, in its governing and defending, in the lives of all its residents, in its situation in the larger world of people and nature. We affirm that God has power to act on our behalf, and we confirm our own responsibility to touch and mingle with, to wrestle and transform the world and society of which we are a part. When we sprinkle its pavements and buildings with the water of baptism, we recall the Holy Spirit brooding on the face of the original deep. We remember God's saving power leading a small captive people across the river separating bondage from freedom, passivity from responsibility, anonymity from vocation as the people of God. We celebrate the way in which we have been made new, reborn by water and the Spirit into a new creation leaning into the radiance of God's promise, out of death into life. We desire with our whole hearts the same renewal for our city and our neighbors as we have known by grace. And as I reminded you last week, we "pray in order to become that for which we pray" (Paul Gibson); we pray to learn how to see with new eyes, with the eyes of Christ, that hidden radiance of the Holy Spirit in all things and especially in one another. We see, in the words of Maximus the Confessor, "a world drenched with Deity, a world of which it is possible to say, 'the Word of God, who is God, wills in all things and at all times to work the mystery of his embodiment.'"[3]

The First Letter of John makes the bold assertion that perfect love casts out fear. We hunger to know just what that is like for ourselves. Jesus perhaps gives it

---

[3] Maximus the Confessor, *Philosophical and Theological Questions*, V.1., ed. D. Staniloe (Athens, 1978), p.248-9.

more concreteness in teaching that the greatest love is that by which a person lays down their life for their friends. And as Jesus loved his friends . . . and all of us . . . with that love, his own fear was indeed cast out. If Jesus was human, he *did* have fear, but it could not paralyze him or overmaster his love, and therefore fell away. Jesus laid down his life not as "victim" in our modern parlance, but as an agent choosing out of his great love for us, his friends. Now in the strength of the Spirit of God which is in us, we also are called to love, not being stopped by our fear.

There is much in the city to make us afraid—the violence close beneath the surface, the kind of indifferent victimization that stressed residents inflict on one another out of their own fear or rage or frustration, or avarice; the abuse of power by those in authority. The cost of failure is high here, and many fear the loss of the basic elements of security: work, home, sustaining relationships. And at times we fear our own potential failure at those important tasks we undertake as a community: will we fall short of what we need to raise to care for our buildings and common life? Will conflict divide us? Will all those people we love leave us and move away? Love bids us move past our fear. Love bids us hold fast to a vision of our unity and connection with God, with each other, and with the whole fabric of creation which holds us. We have been hurt in the past and we may suffer again in the future, but fear no longer has dominion over us; fear does not prevent our loving. Fear does not prevent our hoping and moving forward. Fear does not prevent our raising our hands and voices in praising God.

When we bless—a building, a person, a relationship, an icon, whatever—we do not work magic; that is, we do not seek to manipulate the world, natural or supernatural, according to our own devices and desires, to bend it to our will. Rather, we recognize the love of God intrinsic in the stuff of our lives and in ourselves—the fire in the flint and steel of it—and we lift up our hands and our voices to give thanks to its Author, Light from Light! We and God together do this work of hallowing, of making whole, healthy, and holy, as we open ourselves and our world to the Holy One, receiving blessing from the open hands of God and giving blessing back, in the offering of our praise. In our praying, through the blessing of God, the world is transformed into nearer and nearer likeness to God. We see God sparkle in and through the matter of the universe, and the holy child in us laughs with delight! "These things I have spoken to you," says Jesus, "that my joy may be in you and that your joy may be full."

We cannot accomplish such transformation by ourselves. "We seek what is beyond us, but our desire remains baffled. We are thrown back on ourselves by the enigmas of sin and suffering, of frustration and death. Of ourselves, we cannot attain the goal for which we long. It is only when another comes out from the unknown world of eternity to meet us, and opens to us the way through, that we can find the fulfillment of the desire which we know within ourselves. In Christ God . . . comes out to meet us and becomes the way which leads into the reign of heaven."[4]

So as you walk the city streets today, as you sing, and as you pause for prayer, look. Look, in the loveliness of the world, in the unquenchable green fire of

---

[4]A.M.Allchin, *Participation In God* (Wilton: Morehouse-Barlow, 1988), p. 11.

Spring, in the heart of the city where the rubbing together of human lives sparks compassion. Look! It is Love, Loveself, coming to meet us—Love whose beloved we are—coming to meet us with outstretched arms! Let us love as we are loved. Let us bless as we are blessed.

The Rev. Jennifer M. Phillips

A Social Center for Spiritual Discernment

Anglican Spirituality has always had a social center. It has been the consistent witness of the spiritual mothers and fathers in this tradition that, while relationship with God is always *personal*, it is never *private*. It is only in a sacred covenant community in which we find "personal relationship through Jesus"; and it is only for *celebration in* and the *upbuilding* of such a community that God's saving work is ultimately poured out. This our tradition has always insisted. John Donne's line (slightly altered) captures the spirit succinctly: "No (one) is an island."

The sermons in the final section focus not so much on seasons, special days, sacraments, or sacred metaphors, as they do on spiritual fulfillment in the context of communal spiritual responsibility.

At first glance, **James Bradley's** retelling of the parable of "The Prodigal Son," with relevant first-person references, might seem to be simply a testimony of and exhortation to individual, personal conversion. But read it again more closely—especially the last half.

Similarly, **Richard Belser's** sermon—which is explicitly concerned with the agonizing process of waiting upon God for spiritual discernment—has some resonance with the current popular language of individual psychotherapeutic self-actualization theory. Again, however—read it more closely. Is Belser accommodating to such language, or employing it for deeper purposes—and in the process, even subverting the secular limitations of that language? Let your own reading decide.

The next two sermons tackle thorny ecclesiastical issues. How do you preach on Stewardship Sunday? How do we respond to the evangelism strategies manifested in a Billy Graham crusade? And what does our tradition have to say to its own members—what words of comfort and challenge—when the Anglican ethos that has characterized our understanding of worship, community, and mission, is clearly not in line, either with secular culture or with the currently swelling tides of more conservative evangelical religious traditions?

In the sermons of **Bruce Shortell** and **Andrew Hamersley** you will find thoughtful, self-critical, non-defensive celebrations of community that reverence social-centeredness, but steadfastly refuse to claim their experience of it as invulnerable or self-sufficient.

The last two sermons, by **Linda Clader** and **Jane Sigloh**, focus our sense of socially centered spirituality out beyond the confines of the institutional church. How does a socially centered spirituality ultimately invite us to repentance, self-sacrifice, vulnerability, and radical obedience to the inscrutable wind of God's empowering Spirit? Turn yourself loose to the power of these two sermons, and see where God takes you!

The Man and His Two Sons

"There was a man who had two sons."

Jesus' story is very simple. A man had two sons. The younger son was full of longing and wanderlust. He asked for his inheritance and he left home. Things didn't work out the way he had hoped. All his dreams were shattered. He ended up lost and humiliated. Then he came to his senses and went home, hoping to be able to live as a servant in his father's house. But his father was so glad to see him that he forgave him for all his misdeeds and welcomed him home like a royal guest. And the elder son, the one who never left, who never was frivolous or thoughtless . . . the one who was always faithful . . . that son was upset by his father's generosity to the wayward son. And his father told him, "Your brother who was like dead is now alive. Can you not be joyous?"

That's the whole parable.

It seems so simple, and yet it is so profoundly complicated.

This is such a complex parable because it is not about a father and two sons. It is about you. It is about me. It is about "how we are," "what we're like." It is a parable of the human soul.

Just about seven years ago, I was more confused and troubled than I'd ever been in my life. I was separated from my wife and family. I was living alone. I was not practicing my priesthood. I had told the Bishop I wouldn't function as a priest before he could tell me not to. Most of my friends were nervous around me. Everyone else avoided me.

You see, I know what it's like to be that younger son.

I know what it's like to tend the pigs and hunger for their food.

I know what that's like.

We miss the whole point of this parable if we're too moral about it.

That younger son wasn't a "bad boy." He was just bored. He just had some dreams he didn't think he could ever have at home. He wanted something "more" . . . something more . . .

He looked at his life and realized that everything he had ever done was for someone else. He was bigger than his father's farm. He knew he was! There was the whole world out there to explore. He wanted out. He wanted to be free. He wanted to chase his dream.

So he went to his father and said, "Give me what is mine. Don't make me wait for my inheritance. Give it to me now so I can live and be free."

There's not a parent who ever lived who didn't have nightmares about that moment. There's not a parent who ever lived who didn't dread and fear the time when their child would outgrow them.

That father in Jesus' parable had held that young man in his arms as a baby. That father had soothed his son in the deep night a thousand times. That father had seen his child learn to walk, had wanted to catch him when he stumbled, and had let him fall instead, feeling his own heart break. That father had tended to the wounds and stayed awake through the childhood illnesses and done all he could to teach his son values and manners and what it meant to be a man.

Oh, he had failed. There are no parents who ever lived who haven't failed their children. But he had done what he could do. He had tried. He had tried.

And now, all the laughter and joy of being a parent . . . and all the worry and anguish of parenthood . . . all of it—tears and wonder, longing and trying—all of it was called into question.

"Give me what is mine," his son said to him, "I want to be free of you and of this life."

There must have been a chill that ran over that man's body. This was his worst fear. This child of his wanted to leave.

And the father let him go.

Letting go of what you love—of whom you love—is the hardest thing in the world to do. And the best thing that can be done.

Maybe he argued with his son. Maybe he tried to reason. Maybe he tried to compromise. We don't know. Jesus doesn't tell us. And in the end, he gave his son the inheritance and watched him leave.

Anyone who ever had a child knows what that is like.

It is the hardest thing of all to do. And the most necessary.

This is a parable about the human soul.

It is about "being right" and "looking good."

Back there seven years ago, at the lowest point of my life, I heard someone say that the two things that drive human beings are "being right" and "looking good!"

When I heard that, I realized that those were my "abiding sins." Being right and looking good were my abiding sins.

An abiding sin is one that just won't go away.

It "abides." It stays with you. You just can't get away.

71

The younger son threw all that money away. He poured it down the hole of his own needs and longings. And when it was gone, he was sitting in a pig pen, envying the pigs their food.

It was at that point, sitting in the pig pen, that Jesus tells us that the younger son "came to himself."

That idiom, that saying, "when he came to himself," is, in Greek, a medical term. What the Greek words imply is something like: "when he came to his senses after fainting."

It was like "waking up." The young man "woke up." And when he did, he realized he "wasn't right" and he didn't "look good."

The Hindus call it "sleep," what you and I call "reality." And the Hindus say, "lucky is the person who wakes up before they die."

How lucky that young man was. How fortunate for him that he had hit the bottom. He "came to himself." He "woke up" before he died.

"Being right" didn't matter anymore. "Looking good" was foolish. He was hungry and decided to go home.

He prepared a little speech: "Father, I have sinned before heaven and against you. I am not worthy to be your son. Let me be a servant in your house."

But when he got home, his father didn't even listen to his speech. His father ran meet him. His father dressed him in fine clothing. His father declared a holiday and killed the fatted calf and broke out the good wine. There was to be a celebration. His son who was dead was alive.

Nothing else mattered.

Then the older son showed up. A party was about to start and he was fit to be tied.

"How can you do this to me," he said to his father. "That rascal son of yours has wasted everything and you kill the fatted calf for him. And I've always been good and you've done nothing for me. How can you do this to me. It isn't fair."

The older son was "right." And he "looked good." And it wasn't his party.

He was "right." He "looked good." And it wasn't his party.

Is there anyone here—anyone—who hasn't been the older son from time to time?

Is there anyone here who hasn't experienced "being right" and "looking good" and yet not had a party?

Is there anyone here who hasn't felt that "life isn't fair" from time to time? Anyone here who hasn't felt that?

Stand up if you haven't . . .

This is a parable about "how we are" and "what we're like". It is a parable about you and about me.

This is a parable about our souls.

We have to stop "being right." We have to stop "looking good." We simply have to stop.

All that "being right" gets you is having someone else "be wrong."

All that "looking good" gets you is having someone else "look bad."

That's all there is to it. That's the only payoff. That's all you get. That's it!

In Arthur Miller's play, *After the Fall,* one of the characters says, "I dreamed I had a child, and even in the dream I saw it was my life, and it was an idiot, and I ran away. But it always crept on to my lap again, clutched at my clothes. Until I thought, if I could kiss it, whatever in it was my own, perhaps I could sleep. And I bent to its broken face, and it was horrible but I kissed it. I think one must finally take one's life in one's arms . . . "

All the older son needs to do to go to the party is stop "being right" and "looking good."

All he needs to do is to embrace his brother, his shadow side.

And all we have to do to go to the party is "take our lives into our arms," embrace our shadow side, stop thinking that "being right" and "looking good" will work.

The parable ends with the father going in to the party and the older brother standing outside the door.

That's where we stand right now. This is a parable about our souls.

The fatted calf has been killed. The finest wine has been poured. The party is already begun.

Are we ready to "take our lives in our arms?" Are we ready to embrace the "younger son" of our souls . . . .

Are we ready?

Are we . . . are we really . . . .

The Rev. James Bradley

Floating A Leaf

Restless. Vaguely dissatisfied with the circumstances of life. Trying to feel grateful for blessings, but wondering more and more if something's missing. Sensing that the stream of life has widened into a lake of familiar habit, and feeling out of touch with whatever current brought us where we are. Beloved, if those words describe you, it's time to float a leaf. Let me tell you what I mean.

Some years ago, a friend and I were boating the twisting channel of the Edisto River just south of Orangeburg. It was spring, and the water was high, spilling over the normal river banks to flood large tracts of lowland swamp. But even though the current flowed swiftly between the overhanging trees that still defined the river channel, masses of floating water hyacinth had jammed into every bend in the river, sometimes blocking the channel for 100 yards. After several exhausting efforts to paddle or drag our boat through the water weeds, my friend and I decided it would be easier if we would cut through the flooded forest and follow the moving water in order to meet the river channel around the bend beyond the weeds. The plan worked several times. But then things got complicated.

On the third or fourth shortcut, we were 200 yards into the flooded swamp paddling through a stand of massive cypress trees and admiring the eerie grandeur of the place, when we realized there was no discernible current. The flooded forest had become a vast lake. And every direction looked the same. We began to feel anxious, because the hour was late, and we really didn't want to spend the night in our boat in the swamp. We paddled with growing desperation through the trees in one direction, then, arguing with each other, we'd try another way, hoping to find the river channel before it got dark. Finally, as we slumped exhausted in the motionless boat, my friend reached out and plucked a leaf from one of the bushes we'd been paddling through. He dropped it in the black swamp water. It was a gesture of total defeat. But as we watched, that floating leaf turned slowly and moved away from our boat. My friend and I looked at each other with renewed hope! That leaf was responding to a current we couldn't see, an invisible movement too gentle to pull our boat through the trees. But it took the leaf! And we knew in an instant it was flowing toward the river channel. For the next half hour we'd push between trees, and float another leaf, watch it for a minute, then move expectantly after it. And before long we saw a break in the trees ahead. It was the river channel flowing with a wonderful energy. We pushed out of the forest into the moving water and celebrated.

That's how I first learned to float a leaf. But since then, I've discovered there are other ways to apply this bit of navigational knowledge. I began this morning by describing feelings that many people have when they sense they've lost contact with anything like a meaningful current in their lives. I don't suggest that we're not busy when we begin to feel that way. Ask most of us "What's going on with you?" and often the response begins with a sigh. "Where do I start?" When someone's important goals in life have multiplied and broadened—like a river that's so full it spills over its banks and naturally spreads out into a lake, becoming wider and shallower—when this happens we often don't realize for quite a while that we're not making progress. Like my friend and me paddling unknowingly into the swamp—we were working hard, getting tired, and going nowhere. And that describes many of us—working hard at things we've chosen or things dealt to us, feeling weary and wondering where it all leads. Perhaps we remember when there was a more clearly defined channel for our lives, a sense of direction that pulled us along between recognizable banks. We would mark our progress—like counting bends in the river: at this bend we graduated; downstream a ways we married; a few more turns and children began to join us in the boat; then we passed major events that had to do with a new career or a change of address. All this happened as we prayed for God's blessing and felt swept along by developments we hoped were from him.

And then comes a time when the sense of forward motion begins to diminish. The scenery looks the same, no matter which way we go. And we're in what appears to be still water! It's not an unpleasant place to be at first. We welcome the quiet lake we've entered. We're free to try some different directions for the first time, now that we're not being pulled along by fast moving decisions. But before long, the restlessness begins. We are grateful for all that's happened to get us where we are, but we can't deny a vague dissatisfaction. As frantic as things were when we were in the fast moving current, we find that paddling around and around in a lake that's got a predictable shoreline and a very shallow bottom gets old pretty soon. And then we go searching for fast water again—something to restore a feeling of purpose and movement.

Some people remember the thrill of falling in love. It's like whitewater rafting! And in order to recapture that exhilarating experience, a growing number of people leave marriages that have gotten wider and shallower over the years, and they climb into somebody else's boat. It's exciting, for a while, but when that rushing current slows down, as it always does, then it's easier to jump ship again and again. Others of us change jobs or houses, or both, and the challenges of all that newness quickens the life-current for a while. Travel is a wonderful way to pick up the pace and recapture the feeling that we're going somewhere. We must be going somewhere; we're always packing suitcases! But when the diversions of seven continents begin to look and feel the same, then we're up against the unavoidable truth. We've never really left the lake. We've just paddled hard in a dozen directions, and that deep urgent flow, that sense of movement and meaningful discovery we've longed for, has not been found.

Let me step out of this metaphor for a minute and say it directly. Our lives are often long on activity and short on purpose—real purpose—promising a future larger than our own imaginations. People lacking this sense of direction are vulnerable to all kinds of temptations. And underneath our efforts to find something worthwhile to do with ourselves lies the horrible suspicion that there isn't any deeper meaning—that it's only our choices that briefly satisfy, and it's a waste of time trying to be part of a destiny larger than our own happiness. So what we choose really doesn't matter. We're only staying ahead of underlying chaos.

Perhaps you're not even close to such a state of mind. Maybe you're making real progress and feeling good about things, or perhaps you're paddling in circles and telling yourself that things are fine. But if the day comes when you feel as though something is missing and your life is a circle instead of a line, a lake instead of a river, let me urge you to climb back into my metaphor and float a leaf. To float a leaf is to place on the confusing water around you a prayer for God's guidance. Instead of launching out on a grand scheme of our own and praying, "Lord, let me find the flow of real life in this direction!" stop paddling for a while, and pray, and wait, and watch that prayer turning gently in the current of life around you—watch where that prayer will lead.

The truth that makes me confident about suggesting this is not some extrapolation from hidden river currents to the secret movements of life. I'm basing this on God's promise to Isaiah. Long ago the prophet said, "God created the heavens and formed the earth. God did not create a chaos." This means that under the surface of every human life—stagnant as it may seem— there is a current—the stream of God's will silently tugging at every one of us, saying softly, "Come this way! Here is truth, and life, and joy!" Then we pray by floating a leaf, we're looking to place ourselves in the flow of that divine stream, and no longer begging God to direct the current of creation through channels we've dug for ourselves. The author of Psalm 33 understood this. "God frustrates the plans of the peoples," he wrote. Do we wonder why we get so tired looking for satisfaction on our own terms and so seldom have our prayers answered? We're paddling our own way—ignoring the current that flows from God.

Well, it's fair to ask it: "If we float a leaf, how do we know when we begin to move with the current God sends?" We know when the course of our life begins to look like Jesus' life! You see, he stayed in the main channel of his father's love, and he didn't keep it a secret. He didn't puff people up by saying, as some treacherous voices imply today, "Exert your individuality!" "Magnify your uniqueness!" "Do your own thing!" "Make your Father proud by your fearless initiative!" Jesus told us how to live and promised us power to follow in faith. Calling us his friends, he said, "As the Father has loved me, so I have loved you. Abide in my love. And love one another." Don't go wandering out of the channel. Keep my commandments and you will stay within the current God sends. When the tides of culture are running high and ethical choices have flooded the established channels of morality, the world says, "Hooray! We're free of any restraint! We can paddle wherever we want!" But Jesus told us his word will be for us an invisible and absolutely reliable current. Stay within this silent river and you'll abide in his love and the life-giving flow of the Father will draw you to himself.

It's true that individuals in search of real life can float a leaf—place one prayer after another on the confusing water around them and expect God's silent flow to give direction. And churches can do the same thing—as this congregation is doing between Easter and Pentecost. Finding ourselves in a wide place in the long river of our history, with the culture inviting religious expression in a multitude of false channels, we're floating leaves, hundreds of them. We're praying, "Lord, show us where your current flows for us today," and we'll watch together to discern where the movement of those leaves (those prayers) will lead us. We'll know when we begin to move in the stream of God's will, because our life together will be like our Lord's. It will be faithful to the Father's Word, unconcerned about our own survival, devoted to the well-being of others to the glory of Christ's Name. Can you feel the tug of that current? Float a leaf and watch and listen. Where will the next bend in the river take this church? Beloved, downstream there's joy!

The Rev. Richard I.H. Belser

Evangelism: Episcopal Style

Since last Wednesday evening the Billy Graham Crusade has been going on at the Georgia Dome. The last service is this afternoon at four o'clock. As far as I can tell a few hundred people from the Cathedral Parish have attended. My wife Joyce and I attended on Wednesday and Thursday evenings. Members that I have talked to have felt a good spirit at the Dome—they report that it was powerful and some were moved. Some even went down to the floor of the Dome for the altar call while the choir sang the traditional hymn at a Billy Graham Crusade—"Just As I Am."

However, Billy Graham's evangelism style and his altar call raise questions in the minds of many Episcopalians. It has prompted many to ask, "What is the evangelism style of Episcopalians? How does it differ?" "Do we do that?" somebody asked as people were moving down towards the floor of the Dome. "We don't have an altar call," they said.

We've been in the Decade of Evangelism for at least four years now and many are still turned off by certain evangelism methods. Dwight L. Moody was a well known evangelist. One day a woman came up to him and criticized his method of evangelism and Moody's reply was, " I agree with you. I don't like the way I do it either." "Tell me," he asked her, "how do you do it?" The lady replied, "I don't do it." And Moody said, "Then I like the way I'm doing it better than the way you are not doing it."

Now I'm not one who advocates just any old means to a justified end. There are some methods of evangelism that I have real problems with. For instance, I don't like the "threat technique," or the "fear method" when evangelists threaten hell and punishment if you don't accept Jesus. I don't think Jesus really threatened anyone, though he reminded them of the consequences of their decisions. Rather, Jesus seemed to draw people to him offering love and life.

The conversions that are based on fear and threat I call "shotgun conversions," recalling the old shot-gun marriages. Remember if the girl got pregnant, the irate father found the boy, led him to the marriage altar with the shotgun to his head and said to the boy, "You are going to marry my daughter, aren't you?" "Yes sir!" he replied. "And you are going to love her and care for her and the baby, right?" "Yes sir!" . . . As long as that gun was to the head. But later those marriages were often painful and many broke up.

"Shot-gun conversions" often have similar results. Accepting Jesus while under the threat of hell can bring forth a "yes" but often experience little of God's love and many don't last.

Evangelism methods differ among denominations but the greatest error is to "throw out the baby with the bath water." That is, we cannot stop doing evangelism because we don't like somebody else's methods. We tend to dislike "fundamentalism" and in the process throw out the "fundamentals" of our faith—of our call by Christ to share the good news of his love so that people can experience that love in relationship with him. We are called not just to programs that feed their stomach (as good as those are and as much as we need to do that) but to share his love that invites people to experience his love and presence in soul and spirit.

Fundamentalism to me is not so much a denomination as it is an attitude of legalism—people being narrow, rigid, exclusive, without much grace and without much love. But the fundamentals of our faith are very clear for us in the Bible, in the creed, in the Book of Common Prayer, in our liturgy, and in our music. These fundamentals are best understood, I believe, in the language of relationships.

Before his conversion, a man said, he wanted only about three dollars worth of God. Now, that's not much of a relationship. The result of sin is separation—separation from a relationship with God. The commandments we heard read today from Deuteronomy and St. Mark to love God and love neighbor seem to me to probe each of us—and encourage us to say "yes" to welcoming all of God and offering him all of us.

And so, for me, evangelism "invites" people to take part in the relationship that is healed by Jesus Christ on the cross.

Evangelism is proclaiming by action, but also by word, the Good News that he invites us back into this relationship from which we have wandered.

But that invitation brings us to the next question which often comes up when we start comparing methods—"Do we have to decide to accept Jesus?" There are those that cringe at the old hymn, "I Have Decided to Follow Jesus." And yet, our lives are made up of decisions and in a relationship isn't it true that if there is no opportunity to say "no" to the relationship then "yes" is very empty. The problem with shotgun marriages is, of course, there's no opportunity for the young man to say "no" and therefore the "yes" *is* empty.

Are decisions part of our response to hearing the Good News of Christ? I think so. Jesus asked his disciples, "Who do you say that I am?" He asked for a decision. A prophet . . . a teacher . . . a good man . . . ? Or the Son of God, Savior and Lord? And he invites everyone to decide—not forcing them and not taking away the free choice.

I was counseling a woman in my office some time ago. She had been very injured and abused. Her psychologist sent her to me because she had received much of her hurt from church officials and obviously and understandably no longer trusted God. As we talked she said something that encouraged me to point to a print that hangs on my office wall. It is a painting from St. Paul's Church in London and the print is an illustration of Jesus standing at a door knocking. She looked at it only for a moment and declared, "There's no handle on Jesus' side of the door. We have to open it from the inside." And then she paused, this abused woman, and whispered, "Jesus respects boundaries. Jesus respects boundaries." We must make a decision whether or not to accept his invitation.

Jesus died for everyone but he encourages us to decide to receive what he offers. I believe we need to consciously say "yes"—to RSVP his invitation. And, as Episcopalians, our sacraments can help or they can get in the way. I was baptized as an infant and I remember nothing about it. We have great evangelism opportunities in our sacraments. Both Baptism and Confirmation proclaim the gospel and invite us to decide for Christ, but if we are not consciously aware of our decision, in those sacraments, we lose the peace which comes from knowing we accepted Christ's invitation.

In our Baptism service there is a portion there on that page that has three renunciations—renouncing evil and Satan and sin. That is, an invitation to repent! Then there are three affirmations in the form of questions seeking a decision. "Do you turn to Jesus Christ and accept him as your Savior?" "I do." (Or, "I do not.") "Do you put your whole trust in his grace and love?" "I do." (Or, "I do not.") "Do you promise to follow and obey him as your Lord?" "I do." (Or, "I do not.")

Sounds very much, doesn't it, like the elements in the prayer Billy Graham prays with those who come forward in his altar call. We are not often aware of them because we don't always at the time of Baptism and Confirmation make them very intentional. But it is all there in the prayer book. We can easily get caught up in the words and the actions and not personally acknowledge our choice of accepting what God offers.

And then, in the Confirmation service the same elements are present but more briefly stated. This is when we appropriate our baptismal promises. Bishop Allen, at a diocesan council a few years ago, said, "We need to appropriate for ourselves the baptismal promises." And so, at the Confirmation service he says to the candidates, "Do you reaffirm your renunciation of evil?" (That is, do you repent?) "I do." "Do you renew your commitment to Jesus Christ?" (That's conversion.) "I do. And with God's grace will follow him as my Savior and my Lord."

You see, since the Graham crusade, I suspect that at the office and at home and at parties you are talking about various ways evangelism is done in different denominations. Episcopalians have all of the fundamentals in our own denomination. Our error, I believe, is that we are not always intentional and personal when we bring people to Baptism and Confirmation. Maybe we've thrown out other people's methods and forgotten to use our own method. That may mean, for instance, that some of you do not remember being intentional about deciding to accept Christ's love and forgiveness. You may wonder if you are really in that relationship with Christ that has an eternal quality to it.

I remember a friend of mine once asked a group of people, "How many of you know if you are married or not?" Obvious question, isn't it? Because we remember the decision made at a marriage service and we remember the date of that marriage. If you're not sure, look at the baptismal promises on page 302. Know when you said "Yes." Read them over, personalize them. Say them to the Lord. Let God and you know that you are in that relationship.

You see, some say that there's a "moment of conversion" and some say it is a "process of conversion." I like being an Anglican—I consider it's both. It is not an either/or. For me it goes back to relationship—like in a marriage. There's a time of dating, of getting to know one another. It is a good and valuable time. And then there's a time of decision—the couple has to say yes or no to each other. And if they say yes, then there's a wedding—a date—to remember. It is a time of commitment made to each other for life. And after marriage we all know there's a time of continued growth and commitment because the process of being married continues; it doesn't all happen at the altar.

And so it is, I believe, with our relationship with Christ. A time of dating that is good and valid. And then a decision—a time of commitment—a moment of conversion! Maybe at Baptism. Maybe at Confirmation. Maybe some other time. Maybe today. And then, a long process of conversion in our relationship with the Lord throughout our lives.

When I was in Delaware, whenever someone new came to our congregation we encouraged them to be intentional about their decision to accept the relationship with Jesus Christ. If they were unsure, we urged them to take as much time as necessary; ask as many questions and go to as many classes as you want. But sometime make a choice.

There was a woman who had been attending about a year and a half. As a parish we had decided to paint some older person's home, and she and I happened to be painting the windows up on a roof. We took a break, and while we were sitting there on the roof she came over to me and said, "I'm ready." I said, "For what?" She said, "You know, to make that decision. To make that commitment." I said, "Now?" And she said, "Yeah." And so I said, "Okay," and we said a prayer there on the roof. That was her "altar call" and moment of conversion.

What is our altar call? It is Baptism and Confirmation and it is right here—every Sunday! We have a great altar call. Every Sunday morning when you and I make the decision to step out of that pew and walk down this aisle and come to this altar rail and hold up your hands and say, "I receive you, Jesus. Your body. Your blood. Into my life."

What a tremendous altar call we have. Every Sunday we decide to come forward to drink his blood and to receive his body. Receive him into our lives.

We come forth for many reasons to receive him at the rail. But sometimes it is worth being intentional about our decision to receive Jesus as Savior and Lord. Deciding to follow him. Trusting in his grace and love. It's our altar call. For some it is a first time moment of conversion; for others, part of the ongoing process of conversion.

And as you receive today you might want to say a silent prayer. "I receive you, Jesus, into my life." For most of us it will be a recommitment, like we do every Sunday. For some of you it will be saying, "I receive you," but I need to think about this commitment a little longer. And for some, you will say, I want to know I decided to accept the love and relationship with Jesus and so "I received you into my life right now." Make it intentional. If you do do it for the first time today, please call me or one of the other clergy.

You see, as Episcopalians, we have our way of doing evangelism. Our way of encouraging people to receive the love that Christ offers and our altar calls. We just need to be more intentional about it. I hope this helps you understand and respond to your own conversion and as you talk with other people at the office and at home.

I'd like to conclude with a story from C. S. Lewis. He tells the story of his own conversion and the results. He wrote in *Surprised by Joy*, "You must picture me alone in that room in Magdalene, night after night, feeling whenever my mind lifted even for a second from my work the steady unrelenting approach of Him whom I desired so earnestly not to meet. That which I had greatly feared had at last come upon me. In the Trinity term of 1929 I gave in and admitted that God was God and knelt and prayed. Perhaps that night the most dejected and reluctant convert in all England. I did not then see what is now the most shining and obvious thing. The divine humility which will accept a convert, even on such terms. The Prodigal Son at least walked home on his own two feet. But who can adore the love of him who will open the high gates to a prodigal who was brought in kicking and struggling, resentful and darting his eyes in every direction for a chance to escape. The words 'compel them to come in' have been so abused by wicked men that we shudder at them. But properly understood, they plumb the depth of divine mercy. The hardness of God is kinder than the softness of men. His compulsion is our liberation."

God's invitation abounds. Today's service offers many opportunities for all of us to respond. For a first time—or continuing to respond to that invitation that is extended to us from the cross on that first Easter Sunday. Amen.

© The Rev. Bruce M. Shortell

Loyalty Sunday

Being the Church: Holding on and Letting Go

Last week, our senior warden, Edge Bagg, preached what I thought was an excellent, thought-provoking, and heartfelt sermon. During the course of what he had to say, he mentioned that this week, today, he would be returning to the parish where he grew up, where he was an altar boy and was married, as that parish closed its doors after celebrating its final Eucharist as an Episcopal Church. Calvary Episcopal Church in Utica was founded in the mid-1800s as an alternative to the bigger, fancier, downtown church. Today, it sits in a blighted neighborhood full of vacant lots and boarded-up houses.

This past Monday, Edge and I went to Utica, returning to his church, to walk that holy ground. I knew that this would be a sad experience for him, but I had no idea how large and profound an experience I would have. The church itself is a rare beauty. There are stunning appointments: a fabulous hand-carved marble altar and credence shelf, exquisite stained glass, probably worth millions, wooden pews with carved crosses at their end, and a substantial pipe organ. Walking around the inside of that sacred place, running my hands along the carved altar and standing next to the prayer desk of countless rectors, I found myself in deep mourning. From a priest's perspective, I thought of all those rectors and all their worries. I thought of the genuine tears they shed as they prayed for the welfare of their people. I thought of the joy that they must have shared and the laughter that must have filled those walls. And then I thought of the closing of that church and the heart wrenching challenge of letting all of that go.

This was not an occasion for easy answers or much conversation. Our senior warden is a quiet, deep, and thoughtful man, full of heart and decency, and I felt that my role was most appropriately one of companion and not so much one of counselor. But eventually we did do some talking, and we have talked since and we know that we will need to talk some more.

Among the first things we experienced was the thick sadness of the cold and empty place and its proud but lonely beauty. I told Edge about my sense of the years of faithful priests and their tears and laughter. I expressed my awe at the beauty all around, and how I saw all of it as an offering to God: all that craftsmanship, all that priestly devotion, all those generations of layfolk who put their trust in God and exercised their own ministries. I saw all of those things, all together, as a giant faithful offering that was now over. The proper for All Saints' Day, especially the Old Testament lesson, kept echoing in my head. In Ecclesiasticus it says of the faithful, "Some of them have left behind a name, so that others declare their praise. But of others there is no memory; they have perished as if they had never existed . . . But these also were godly men, whose righteous deeds have not been forgotten..." I tried to find words to tell Edge of the faith that all these faithful offerings, those known, and those unknown, are never lost on God. This moment in Utica led me to want to believe with certainty that God receives all that we have to offer and pulls it all together, knitting all those loose threads into God's own mysterious design. I found myself repeating the phrase, "Nothing gets lost."

But there are many layers to this encounter and viewing the parish church and its people, buildings, and life as an offering is just one of them. As we allowed the weight of the moment to settle on us, it became clear that a parish church is not only the vehicle for our offering, it is also a sign of the presence of God in our lives and for our communities. And as a sign, the physical aspect of the church—its vestments, bell tower, altar, organ, pews and stained glass—takes on a holiness all of its own. It is easy for us to imbue these symbols of God's presence and sovereignty with what amounts to an idolatrous power, forgetting, for generations at a time, that they too are mortal and will eventually join with the rest of the dust. But this is an idolatry which is easy to forgive because we just don't want to think about the end of things. It is as if we are children, pretending that our parents will always be there.

Edge may have sounded an alarm last week which some did not want to hear. His experience of the death of his first parish has, I know, given birth to a resolve not to let that happen here. The fact is that our parish is fairly healthy at this moment but certainly not immune from the fate being experienced by Calvary, Utica. And Edge's and my experience of the crumbling of idols brought us, I think, face to face with the mortality of every living thing, including St. Andrew's Church.

I have to tell you that part of my response to these realities is to want to curl up in a ball and weep. To think that all of our efforts, all our meetings, all our caring, all our devotion, all our might could one day not be enough feels like the rug is being pulled right out from under our collective feet. But the harsh and valuable lesson that I take away from this experience, so far anyway, is not finally one of defeat and grief. As we are brought up short in this experience, we stare into two grown-up realities. One is that our offerings to God must be freely given without the hope of reward or the illusion of permanence. The other is that signs of God, no matter how holy, are not God. When we work through these realities, in faith, I think we are then face to face with the kingship or the sovereignty of God.

In one sense this is a lousy stewardship sermon because stewardship is often marketed, with a tacit acknowledgment that God is Lord, but more emphasis on our particular product. I seriously doubt there is any way to avoid that. We want to celebrate our community, our lives together, and God's blessings. We want to motivate people to pledge generously so that we can expand our ministries and keep this good and lively ball rolling. But by allowing some sober existential lessons to infiltrate this moment, we are given the rare opportunity for clarity. We can joyfully acknowledge that we exist for God alone and we exist particularly through the saving death of God's Son to offer our heartfelt lives as freely and obediently as we can manage.

The fact is that God existed perfectly well before St. Andrew's Church in Albany and will exist perfectly well after we are history. But that does not mean that we are irrelevant to God, that we don't have a case to make in our own time, that we don't have our own adventure in faith to live. We do! We can, however, be mature Christians who have seen our own mortality and are there-by made free to act with a boldness of vision, with radical compassion, with exuberant joy, and a deeply humble devotion. If, in 50 or 250 years, some future priest and warden have the great good fortune to come back to this holy dwelling and run their hands over our altar or around the carved angels at the sanctuary steps, or take in the vast beauty of our windows, in the week before *our* doors are closed, let those pilgrims attend our death with the same sense of awe I had this week in Utica! Let it be clear that there were real tears spilled in these pews, real joy shared at this font, glorious music offered in this place, real care extended from this altar, Jesus Christ proclaimed with faith year after year from this pulpit, and his death and resurrection made present week by week in the sacrament. We have, it seems to me, a godly obligation to make sure that somewhere down the line, someone is going to have a *very* hard time with our demise. Meanwhile it is our duty to ensure that our spiritual children are well prepared with a true faith and that they will be able, after what we hope is a *great* struggle, finally to let us go when that time comes. Like any good parent, we hope that we will have taught them the importance of offering their absolute best in service, the importance of giving their gifts without strings, and the joy and wonder that comes with worshiping the King of kings and Lord of lords, who, alone, is God.

The Rev. Andrew Hamersley

Luke 18:1-8

A Woman Whose Name is Justice

I've been a victim of injustice, now and then. Nothing big, you know, just the usual stuff that a woman deals with in a man's world; just the usual stuff that a student deals with in an academic world; just the usual stuff that a seminarian deals with in the world of the church. Some of you have had to deal with a lot more.

I've been a victim of injustice, now and then. And because I've had my own little taste of victimhood, and because I've spent some time around prisons and have come to know and to love a lot of victimizers who are victims themselves, and because I'm a Christian and have made a vow to strive for justice and peace among all people, and respect the dignity of every human being—because of all that, when a widow makes her way from the shadows into the spotlight of a gospel narrative—this widow of the parable, or any widow in scripture (they're all really the same person, in a way)—when a widow walks into a scripture story, I know where I am. I stand at her side. I take her position. I get inside her—and I feel the ache of her hunger, and I feel the shame of her poverty, and I weep the tears of her frustration, the frustration of never having a voice, the frustration of never getting an ear.

And the more actual victims I get to know person-ally, the more my anger energizes my cries of injustice, and the louder I raise my voice against the people, and against the structures that hold the widows of this world captive in their poverty, captive in their power-lessness. And the sound of my own voice—raised in anger—the sound of my own voice is sweet.

It's sweet to join the widow as she badgers that unjust judge. It's sweet to pound my fist for her, and to cry "unfair" for her, to that faceless, shameless bad guy. But today my cries have gotten stuck in my throat, and I seem unable to manage a fist. And I'm confused about that widow and this parable, and what it's all about. Because this week I met a woman whose first name is Justice.* And she didn't look like that bad guy in the parable. In fact, in a number of ways, she looked a lot like me.

Oh, I know that's not what the parable is really doing. I know it's really about prayer, about praying always and not losing heart—that's what Luke tells us it's about—"Jesus told them a parable about their need to pray always and not to lose heart."

But the widow's demand is *justice*. And the object of the praying is *justice*. And try as we might, we just can't seem to get away from the fact that the whole thing—the whole thing—is very much about *justice*. Jesus says so. The prophets say so. Deuteronomy says so: "Justice, and only justice, you shall pursue, so that you may live, and occupy the land that the Lord your God is giving you" (16:20).

But then, of course, actually the parable isn't really about prayer, either, because it turns out that the question it's answering isn't "How do you pray?" or "What do you pray for?" or anything like that. The question it's answering is "When is the kingdom of God coming?" That's the question the story is answering.

---

*Supreme Court Justice Sandra Day O'Conner, who spoke to those attending the Excellence in Preaching Conference.

The Pharisees and the disciples ask when the kingdom will come, and Jesus answers with a parable about praying all the time and not losing hope, with a parable about justice.

And so we have a question about the coming of the kingdom, and we have an answer about prayer, and we have an answer about justice.

And just when you think you may be getting a handle on sorting it all out, how the kingdom and prayer and justice might all connect after all, Jesus says, "Actually, the *real* question is, 'When the Son of Man comes, will he find faith on the earth?'"

Brother and sister preachers, I find the end of this parable a very uncomfortable place to stand. I have no doubt that we preachers are called to take our place by that widow's side, and to add our voices to her pleas for justice. And I have no doubt that we are called not only to shout for justice but to pray for it and to work for it. And I have no doubt that fundamentally, and without ceasing, our prayer must be, "Thy kingdom come."

But everywhere else in the gospel, Jesus assures us that the coming of the kingdom will mean that the humble and meek, the widows of the world, will be exalted. And on the flip side of that assurance is the promise that God will put down the mighty from their seat.

And this is a most uncomfortable place to stand, because in spite of my eagerness to hold that widow's hand and to give my voice to her petitions, in spite of my eagerness to take up arms at her side, I have to remember the experience this week of meeting that woman whose first name is Justice, who is a Christian and an Episcopalian, and who struggles with what that means every day. And when I think about her, I have to realize that I look a lot more like her than like the poor widow.

I had the privilege one summer of sitting in on a course on "Preaching in the African-American Tradition," taught by the Rev. J. Alfred Smith Sr., pastor of Allen Temple Baptist Church in Oakland, California. And one day, well into the course, a rather starry-eyed young white seminarian suddenly saw the light, and exclaimed, "But my congregation will be affluent, white, mainline protestants. They won't be the children of Israel, they'll be the Egyptians. How do I preach to the Egyptians?"

And Pastor Smith was quiet for a moment, and said, "Well, I don't know how to preach to the Egyptians: that's not where my experience has been." And then he smiled. "But fortunately, we have Professor Linda Clader among us this week. She's an *Episcopalian*. She can tell you!"

Let's face it, brother and sister preachers, let's not kid ourselves—when the mighty are laid low, and the humble are exalted, a lot of Episcopalians stand a good chance of being numbered among the formerly mighty. And when the children of Israel are safe on the far side of the Red Sea and the waves are crashing down on Pharaoh's army—a lot of us Episcopalians stand a good chance of getting wet.

So when we preachers stand by that widow's side, and shake our fists at the people and the structures that hold her captive, and preach the kingdom and preach justice—let's be clear about what we are doing. When we take our stand by that widow's side we are taking our stand before the great judgment seat of Christ. Do we have the courage to keep on praying, *anyway*, "Thy kingdom come"? Do we have the courage to keep on preaching justice, *anyway,* knowing that justice for the widow could mean condemnation for us? When the Son of Man comes, will he find *this* kind of faith on the earth?

Exactly this is the gift of the Good News we proclaim: that we can be empowered to risk everything—even to play the fool—trusting in the assurance of God's forgiveness, trusting in the assurance of God's steadfast love.

The Rev. Linda L. Clader

Let It Fly

"Behold I send the promise of my Father upon you; but stay in the city until you are clothed with power from on high." And so they did, going about the routine business of the church. Electing Matthias to take the place of Judas, things like that. All the while pacing the floor and watching the clock.

Then one day it happened. On the Feast of Pentecost they were all together in one place and there was a sound like the rush of a mighty wind. And there appeared to them tongues as of fire, resting on each of them, and they were clothed with power from on high.

And on that same day Peter found the word of God. Beneath all the confusion and denial and guilt and grief he found it! And lifted it up to heaven. And let it fly. It caught the wind, tumbled the tops of trees. "People of Israel, give ear to what I say. This Jesus of Nazareth has been raised from the dead and exalted at the right hand of God and the Holy Spirit has been poured out on us." And the people listened. And their minds were opened to understand the scripture. And when Peter had finished speaking the disciples baptized three thousand people. Now it takes a long time to baptize three thousand. But no one complained. In fact, some said it was the nicest service they had ever been to.

And the word multiplied and prevailed. It spread out beyond the Portico of Solomon to Jerusalem and Judea. It found the voice of Paul and Lydia and even poor bruised Eutycus began to speak and Silas and

Barnabas and Priscilla. "This Jesus of Nazareth has been raised from the dead and the Holy Spirit has been poured out on us."

And the people continually praised God. Well, most of them praised God. There were some who didn't. You see, there were some who were afraid of the power of the word because it can do all sorts of things when you let it fly. It can heal. It can make a straight path out of a crooked one. It can give shelter to the dispossessed and break the back of exclusivity. And it can give hope. Yes, it can give hope even in a world where children have no bread to eat, no water to drink. Even in a world where thousands and thousands of youngsters have track marks on their arms and bottles hidden in brown paper bags. Even in a world where old women have lost all the men in their family to a civil war. It can give hope.

So, of course, the power of the word bothered the authorities in city hall. And they decided to chain it to the prison wall, just as a precaution, you understand, so things wouldn't get out of hand. But while the guards were asleep there was an earthquake and the chains around the word were unfastened. They just dropped to the ground. And the word was free to spread to the ends of the earth and down through the ages.

It dwelt in the voice of Perpetua and Agnes and John Chrysostom. In Boniface of Mainz who gave his life that minds might be opened to understand the scripture. It dwelt in Bernard of Clairvaux and John Donne and Absalom Jones and John Wesley and Phillips Brooks— *lengthily* in Phillips Brooks.

All of these saints straddled the fault line between heaven and earth, bringing their world and God's world together in one breath. And if God said "Go to Nineva and cry against them" they did it. They didn't blink. Like Paul they declared the whole counsel of God. And they told people about forgiveness, how God said it's OK. "No, really, it's OK." And always, always they waited at the foot of the stairs to be clothed with power from on high.

And the word multiplied and prevailed. Until finally it came to rest in pulpit editions—marked with Post It notes for the Sunday reader. Start here. Stop. It came to rest in leather limber bindings held high above the head like the hand of a winner. In study texts and gospel parallels. In little white New Testaments. In single page inserts that trembled in the hand.

And there it remains today. Will it live again in our time? Will it take flight the way it did in the voice of Peter and all the others? Will it tumble the tops of trees and break away from prisons? And will it live in the aftermath, long after the pews have emptied?

I guess we are here at the College of Preachers to answer that question. And the truth is, I don't know the truth. But Toni Morrison poses the same question about language and answers it in a story. Once upon a time there lives an old woman, blind but wise. She is the daughter of a slave and she lives alone in a small house outside of town. Her reputation for wisdom is without peer and without question.

One day the old woman is visited by a group of young people. They enter her house and stand before her. And one of them says "Old woman, I hold in my hand a bird. Tell me, is it living or is it dead? She does not answer and the question is repeated. "Is the bird I am holding living or dead?"

Still she does not answer. She is blind and cannot see her visitors, let alone what is in their hands. Finally she speaks in a voice that is soft but stern. "I don't know," she says, "whether the bird you are holding is dead or alive, but what I do know is that it is in your hands. In *your* hands."

We could talk a lot about what the bird in the story signifies but because we are here at this conference I choose to read it as the word of God and the woman as an ancient preacher who knows that the life of the bird depends on a new generation. "It is your responsibility," she says. "You are its custodians."

So the question stands. Will it live again? Say yes. Say Amen. Take it off the page. Cut the tethers and let it fly. Tell all your people how God molded us into being from the dust on the ground and taught us how to walk and gathered us up in love past all measure. But that was not enough so God became one with us. And lived and died and lived again. Then, even as we disbelieved for joy, that same God clothed us with power from on high.

The world needs to hear that. It's out of tune, out of hope. It is waiting "as at the end of a long winter for one flower to open." It is waiting for you to speak.

The Rev. Jane Sigloh

What Does One Make of Such a Hearing?

Obviously, whatever one choses to make (or feels led to make) of it. Especially since these sermons have been assembled from many different sources, and have subsequently been shaped in relation to each other with the most slender of suggestive commentary, there may be no significant "conclusions" worth putting forward. We would, however, like to venture a few parting reflections.

Even if the categories we have suggested have some credibility in delineating a distinctive flavor for Anglican preaching, it is surely evident that each preacher is his or her own person. This is most clearly evident in the variety of sermon styles that have been presented. Some are rather straightforward arguments, some immerse us in the live action of a story, some shower us with shimmering images. The personality of the preacher is "up front" in some of these sermons. It is clearly recognizable, but at the edges of others. In some of these sermons, one would have to be a member of the congregation to see how the life of the preacher informs the life of the sermon.

For some of these preachers, scripture seems to be only an occasional touchpoint; for others it is a not especially obvious, but subtlety informing heart; for others it is a more or less active companion in the sermon conversation; for still others, scripture is a constant, clearly sounding cadence. Notice, too, how some preachers stay centered in a single text. while others weave a variety of scriptural voices into their sermon tapestries.

Clearly, there is no one way to "do" a sermon in the Episcopal preaching tradition. The way in which season, special day, sacrament, sacred metaphor, and social center for spirituality are interwoven in these sermons is more indicative of the tradition than are matters of sermon style.

Yet a case could credibly be made for claiming that even these designated "distinctives" are not, in fact, unique to the Anglican tradition. One finds them in the preaching of other traditions, probably most explicitly in Lutheran and Roman Catholic churches; less widely, but sometimes quite overtly, in the preaching of Reformed and Methodist traditions. Even some congregations in more "free church" traditions have recently become more sensitive in their preaching to certain of these factors.

The problem here is akin to that of specifying, in formal language, the physical features of persons who share a common biological heritage. There is a "family resemblance" among them that is more or less evident, depending on the characteristics of the different subjects and the sophistication of the observer's perception. Pressing for points is not usually a worthwhile enterprise, unless a special concern is at stake. And yet, spontaneously we say things like: "I knew you were one of the Joneses; you take after your grandfather."

After listening to these sermons, we suspect that you will have a sense, however intuitive or tacit, that there is a family resemblance in the Anglican preaching family—however recessive the homiletical genes may be! This is not to say, of course, that any preacher in this tradition will or should aspire to be "a chip off the old block." Most offspring are at pains to define their individuality in relation to their forebears. There are healthy renegades and rebels in any family.

And yet, whatever it involves, there is something about who and how they are that is manifested in and through members of a family. Shared traits, shared experiences, shared heritage—all of these serve as points of contact when a family gathers at table, or for "reunion."

In a period of tumultuous change, vigorous ideological disagreement, and rancorous partisan debate such as the Episcopal Church is undergoing (along with the rest of society), abstract calls to unity do not cut much ice. One thing we might do with profit, however, is listen more frequently and more deeply to each other when we talk about God. Not just in the "sharing of personal stories" but in those more elevated yet still intimate speech acts where we gather to listen and to preach—to bear witness, thoughtfully and artfully, to the transforming power of God's grace revealed in Jesus Christ.

We may have no healthier way of celebrating the richness of our unity than to attend carefully to one another as we preach. The purpose of this book has been to make that invitation.

Contributions

J. Neil Alexander is Trinity Church Professor of Liturgics and Preaching at The General Theological Seminary in New York.

Richard I. H. Belser is Rector of St. Michael's Church, Charleston, South Carolina.

James Bradley is Rector of St. John's Church, Waterbury, Connecticut.

Glenn E. Busch is Rector of St. Mary's Church, High Point, North Carolina.

Linda Clader is Associate Professor of Homiletics at The Church Divinity School of the Pacific in Berkeley, California.

Barbara Crafton is Associate at The Church of St. John's in the Village, New York.

Edward Garrigan is Rector of St. Paul's Church, Doylestown, Pennsylvania.

Andrew Hamersley is Rector of St. Andrew's Church, Albany, New York.

A. Robert Hirschfeld is Vicar of St. Mark's Chapel, Storrs, Connecticut, and Episcopal Chaplain to the University of Connecticut.

Judith McDaniel is Associate Professor of Homiletics at the Virginia Theological Seminary in Alexandria, Virginia.

Jennifer M. Phillips is Rector of Trinity Parish, St. Louis, Missouri.

Bruce Shortell is Canon for Pastoral Care at The Cathedral of St. Philip in Atlanta, Georgia.

Karen F. Siegfriedt is Pastoral Assistant at St. Luke's Church, Los Gatos, California.

Jane Sigloh is Rector of Emmanuel Church, Staunton, Virginia.

J. Donald Waring is Rector of St. Thomas' Church, Terrace Park, Ohio.

Editors

Roger Alling is President of the Episcopal Evangelism Foundation, which oversees both the annual Preaching Excellence Conference for Episcopal Seminarians and the nationwide call for sermons that are eventually published in this volume. He has previously served as Stewardship Officer for the Diocese of Connecticut. And has served parishes in New York, Pennsylvania and New Jersey.

David J. Schlafer is Adjunct Professor of Homiletics at Virginia Theological Seminary. He has previously served as a professor of preaching at Nashotah House, Seabury-Western, The University of the South, and has been Interim Director of Studies at The College of Preachers. He is the author of *Surviving the Sermon: A Guide to Preaching for Those Who Have to Listen,* and *Your Way with God's Word: Discovering Your Distinctive Preaching Voice,* both published by Cowley Publications. He is currently writing another book for Cowley, *What Makes this Day Different?: Preaching Grace on Special Occasions.*